When Things Begin to Go Bad

Narrative Explorations of Difficult Issues

Edited

George Howard
and
Edward A. Delgado-Romero

Hamilton Books
an imprint of
University Press of America,® Inc.
Dallas · Lanham · Boulder · New York · Oxford

Copyright © 2004 by
Hamilton Books
4501 Forbes Boulevard
Suite 200
Lanham, Maryland 20706
UPA Acquisitions Department (301) 459-3366

PO Box 317
Oxford
OX2 9RU, UK

Library of Congress Control Number: 2004102912
ISBN 0-7618-2865-6 (paperback : alk. ppr.)

Contents

Preface

I've been listening to stories all my life. When I was a child I listened to the stories that my mother told me, especially those stories about her childhood in Colombia, South America. I was enchanted by the tales of my mother as a youth. Through these stories she passed along her beliefs, opinions, fears, prejudices and most of all, her hope. Over time I began telling her stories and they gradually became my own. I also created new stories, stories that told other people who I was, what was important to me, and how I understood the world.

As I grew older other stories and storytellers came into my life, often through music, film, and the written word. Songs provided the soundtrack to my life and having the right music became a lifelong passion. Crowded bookshelves, CD and DVD bins testify to the way that other storytellers have influenced my life.

However, the most influential storytellers were the real people in my life. A good example was Sister Pat. Sister Pat came to my Catholic elementary school when I was in the seventh grade. She looked like no nun I had ever met. She didn't wear a habit or "nun clothes" and had big curly hair. She was full of enthusiasm and energy, especially about the theatre. Sister Pat took a special interest in me and actually convinced me to try acting and singing, despite my obvious lack of talent. I still laugh when I think of introverted me running around a stage singing and acting. I wonder what kind of person I would have become if Sister Pat had more than two years to mold me.

Another important storyteller in my life was George Howard. I met George when I started graduate school at the University of Notre Dame in 1991. But we had met before then. I had met George through the stories he told in Psychology journals. I vividly remember reading his article *Culture Tales* and being struck by the way that George made psychology accessible to everyone, and how he claimed that psychology was one of the many stories that humankind told. The thought that I could merge my love of storytelling with a profession intrigued me.

Before I began graduate school I made contact with George and he gave me copies of his books *A Tale of Two Stories* and *Dare We Create a Human Science*. Reading the fearless way that George would weave his life story alongside the story of science or the story of psychology was exciting. However, I also felt an inequality between George and myself because I knew so much about him and he knew little about me. I wanted to show up the first day of graduate school and hand him a copy of my biography, but I didn't have one. Instead I became a regular in his office and over the course of five years George helped me to tell my story, and create a new one, as I became a counseling psychologist.

I taught a course at Notre Dame using George's book *Understanding Human Nature: An Owner's Manual*. I was amazed at the power of narrative interventions to help first year students at a critical time in their lives as they struggled to tell and then actualize their dreams. I found it exhilarating to help these students understand where they had come from (via autobiographies) and what they wanted to become (through teleographies—imagining ones future).

One student stands out in particular: Jose was from Chicago and I met him on his first day on the Notre Dame campus. He came from a very loving family, but had seen some harsh things in his young life. Jose wanted to get an education, but wasn't sure he could do it, especially at highly competitive school like Notre Dame. Jose wrote a teleography about his life and was able to identify the things about his life that were strengths. Jose had one critical insight when he realized that surviving in the classroom wasn't all that different from the way he had survived in his neighborhood. At Notre Dame ideas and words were the weapons of choice, and the classroom was often a psychological battlefield full of intimidation and gamesmanship. This was something Jose could handle! In his teleography he wrote about his future as a lawyer and family man. I spoke with Jose eight years after he had written his teleography, and after having graduated, spending some time in the workforce, and struggling through some transitions he is now about to enter law school. He was surprised when I mentioned that he had envisioned this path for himself as a first year student. Yet the seeds of his success had been planted long ago.

George and I were talking about how we could work together on some writing projects and he had an inspiration to write a book about topics that are difficult to deal with. This would be a book about complex issues that tend to be avoided—which are exactly the kinds of things that should be shared and discussed. He wrote a short teleography about his dying that set the tone. The story was dark and disturbing, but ultimately about hope. This struck me as the essence of the book. It would be easy enough to write a depressing collection of stories about despair and darkness. The real trick would be to accurately engage difficult issues, but maintain and explore the thread of hope at the same time.

George has been my mentor for the past thirteen years and I'm used to taking directions from him. However, I realized as I was waiting around for him to begin work on this book that there was nothing stopping me from taking the lead on the book. Of course *Tough Topics,* now re-titled as *When Things Begin To Go Bad* is very much guided by the work George has done, but the book also represents an important new phase in my story - the part where I take the lead.

I put out a call to colleagues for first person essays on tough topics. We received chapters over an incredible array of topics. George and I met to discuss the topics and see what would emerge. In general the stories fit under the broad category of dealing with transitions in one's life, either planned or unplanned. These stories represent the author's reactions to being faced with dilemmas and struggling to grow, heal and overcome the problems they encounter. I believe you will be amazed at the variety of tough topics that these authors chose to explore. Finally I trust you will be enriched by the sensitivity and wisdom that all of our contributors bring to their explorations of some of the troubling times and topics of their lives.

My thanks and admiration goes out to the authors of this book, not only for their patience in compiling and editing this volume, but also their willingness to be vulnerable and share their stories. We are all enriched by their work.

Edward Delgado-Romero, Bloomington, Indiana, July 5, 2003

Acknowledgements

We would like to acknowledge the patience of the authors as they have waited several years, often without progress, for this project to become a reality. We are happy to finally be able to share your stories.

We would also like to acknowledge the work of Jessica Barfield and Deleska Crockett as they finished the formatting and indexing of the book.

Introduction: When Things Begin to Go Bad
Edward A. Delgado-Romero & George S. Howard

The human condition condemns all of us to go through some tough times in life—the end of relationships, depression, experiences of racism, affronts to ones self-esteem, physical and psychological abuse, death, betrayal, and many more. The natural tendency to withdraw into a self-protective cocoon is often ones first response. With luck, sufferers will soon begin to articulate their thoughts and feelings to a trusted intimate—ones' partner, a close friend, a spiritual advisor, or a counselor. But doing so is often difficult, as one must overcome the natural impulse to deny or run away from the source of the pain. But is there any doubt that speaking of ones pain is an important step in the process of recovery? Telling ones story is the first step towards giving suffering meaning, and by finding meaning in suffering the healing process can begin. Finding meaning in suffering is one of the oldest human practices and it can be found in mythology, spirituality and religion and ethics. Whether the story is Orpheus descending into Hades, Job's faith being tested, Viktor Frankl surviving a concentration camp, Bill W. compiling the "Big Book" in an attempt to deal with his alcoholism, Mother Teresa working with the poorest of the poor in Calcutta, or Maya Angelou confronting racism: they all find meaning in their suffering. Their stories provide hope and inspiration and help others find meaning in their own suffering.

Modern stories are told over electronic mediums. In television, Oprah Winfrey's talk show is a popular example of sharing stories in order to inspire, motivate and emotionally connect with viewers. In all likelihood, listening to others talk about their struggles in life can help sufferers to feel less isolated and disturbed about their problems. This phenomenon is far more than "misery loving company." Humans are blessed to be able to learn vicariously by witnessing the struggles of others. The philosopher Karl Popper proclaimed, "Humans are the most fortunate of all creatures, for they can die thousands of times in their imagination, rather than once in reality".

However, lately a puzzling contemporary phenomenon has emerged in popular culture: suffering as entertainment. The Jerry Springer Show typifies the type of popular television shows where the misery of others is paraded by people speaking on painful topics such as infidelity, depression, problems with ones kids, and other topics sometimes stretching to the bizarre. Conflicts often escalate into violence. Also popular is "reality" television where contestants are humiliated, endure torturous challenges and make important life decisions (like whom to marry) based on public opinion. The point is not to find meaning in suffering, but rather to amuse or entertain. Many of the stories told on television shows simply demonstrate the messes that people can make of their lives. Apart from feeling ones lot in life—however bad—is certainly better than the circumstances of these poor souls, one wonders what of value a person can take from the more bizarre tales of woe. Suffering as entertainment is not limited to these type of television programs of course, as we live in an era where wars are broadcast live on television, crime is presented as entertainment (Cops, World's Greatest Car Chases), bestselling tabloids feature salacious gossip, and dogmatic radio hosts who berate and belittle the suffering of others.

However, all is not lost. Rather than focusing on suffering as entertainment, we seek through this book to return to the tradition of finding meaning in suffering. People who genuinely believe that they have a worthwhile message to extract from their suffering frequently share their stories or personal narratives with others. The act of sharing those stories demands courage and entails an internal and external risk. Internally the author must live and relive the story to make sense of it, and often this can be painful. Once the author faces and makes sense of their pain they face the external challenge: sharing the story with others and subjecting their story to (hopefully constructive) criticism and public reaction. Sharing ones story provides the possibility of connection and support from others, but rejection and dismissal are real possibilities as well. It takes courage to share ones story, not only because it might be awkward and perhaps unpopular to do so, but also because telling the story also entails giving up privileges—privileges about race, gender, sexual orientation, class, ones profession and perhaps, most of all the privilege not talk about ones suffering. Therefore the editors of this book are indebted to the authors of our chapters, who were willing to take risks to both find meaning in their suffering and to share that meaning with others.

When things begin to go bad is a collection of essays by professionals (e.g., psychologists, therapists, educators) of difficult times they experienced in life. These stories represent the author's reactions to being faced with dilemmas and struggling to grow, heal and overcome the problems they encounter. The reader should note that we did not make a distinction between fact and fiction; these are narratives that are a blend of fiction and non-fiction—the playground of the subjective and the objective. Narratives are invariably co-

constructed in that the reader brings their own life experience and mix it with the narrative of the author. What evolves is a unique experience. In that sense, everything in this book is truth, the author's truth, and perhaps your truth also.

In the first chapter George Howard sets the tone for the book and introduces us to the concept of a teleology – imagining and telling a narrative about ones future – while exploring the possibility of his death. Twelve narratives follow and the final chapter explores the meaning of hope. The stories in this volume are told in a manner designed to normalize the experiences, and to show how others might navigate similar troubled waters in their own lives. Pain and suffering are an inevitable part of the human experience. Reading about how others have turned personal difficulties into growth full experiences can help readers react more constructively at that crucial moment when things begin to go bad in their lives.

Diminished Capacities
George S. Howard

My father often went on long walks. I picked up his habit early, and I knew that walking made us soul mates in some way. However, I never overanalyzed my ambulatory ways—and perhaps I shouldn't do so now. I guess I was simply a walker by nature.

In my mid-twenties I ran daily with a group of friends through the spectacular woods at Duke. But once separated from those friends, I immediately decelerated to a more comfortable pace. Whenever I ran, all I could do was suffer and sweat. While walking, my mind and my mouth both cruise at a comfortable pace—although often far faster than the posted speed limits. Golf courses and college campuses are close to heaven for my jaunts. City streets or country roads will do in a pinch.

I've counseled, consulted, created, cried, consoled, cajoled, cursed and even catastrophized while on long walks. Doing so in my office would have been work—when walking, one can play while one works. Is it not my task in life to meld my avocation with my vocation? Being born to walk, it makes sense to become a mailman, drill instructor, professional golfer, trail guide, waiter, or college professor. Let me see, which of these would I like to become?

Consider the benefits of the habit of taking long walks with friends on physical health, mental health, relationships, spiritual development, life satisfaction, weight, and so forth. How strange that modern society seems hell-bent on reducing the amount that we walk. How successful have you been in making walking a regular activity in your life?

About three years ago I began walking much less. I began to limp as my hip and back started to hurt. I now have a titanium hip due to arthritis, and my walking has declined by about ninety percent. Walking is uncomfortable. My life has been impoverished by this turn of events. The effects of not walking enough are many and depressing. I don't know if this is a temporary condition or if I'll never get back to normal. So that's my problem.

Possible Futures

In addition to writing autobiographies, students in my "Psychology of healthy lifestyles" course are encouraged to write teleographies - that is, possibly true stories of the rest of their lives. Since the future has not yet occurred, my students must be ready to write works of fiction.

Their autobiographies, in contrast, are presumably works of nonfiction. While I generally like the teleographies that my students write, the overwhelming majority are overly optimistic, "My presidential inaugural address harkened back to several themes in my Notre Dame valedictory address..." I constantly urge students to compose more realistic scenarios of their futures, but these exhortations generally fall on deaf ears. Students just don't seem to want to foresee bad things (divorce, business failures, addictions, illness, legal problems) occurring in their lives.

My gut reaction is that overly positive teleographies are probably not as helpful as stories that include some negative events. Are the students' intuitions to "keep it positive" more accurate than my hunches?

The truth is that no one knows for sure, as no research currently exists on the effects that writing a teleography (whether a positive, negative, or a mixed story) has on the remainder of a student's life. We *do* know that taking the "Psychology of healthy lifestyles" course as freshmen enables students to curb their rate of increase in alcohol consumption by 45% from their senior year of high school to the end of their freshman year. However, we don't know exactly which part of the course (e.g., class lectures, discussions, autobiography, teleography) is responsible for the lower levels of alcohol consumption relative to students who do not take the course. In any event, here's a negative teleography of the rest of my life.

"He who hesitates"

Procrastination was never a big problem in my life, but I just never got around to solving my post-surgery problem of not exercising. I knew that strokes were a part of my family history, but until I reached my late 40s, I had always gotten plenty of exercise. I was blessed with low blood pressure (like my father) and weight wasn't a big problem (I was always 212 lbs, but hoping to be 200 lbs—sound familiar?). But since that hip replacement surgery in 1997, I have been unable to get back on any exercise program. I tried walking, but my old habit never came back. My hip (and later my back) always hurt me. I honestly believe that my surgically repaired leg was a little shorter after the operation—but I guess we'll never know. My surgeon wanted me to get into swimming, but by the time my hip healed, that 212 lb physique was a girthy 225 lbs. To be honest, during the final years of the twentieth century I was embarrassed about the way I looked in a bathing suit. (Vanity, thy name is human). So, swimming was a non-starter for me.

For my New Millennium Resolution, I vowed to lower my weight from 248 lbs to 225 lbs—I realized sadly that my days of even hoping for a return to 200 lbs were now behind me. But I knew that I needed to do something soon. To my horror, I would now get a little winded simply by doing cleaning chores—straightening up the living room, carrying out the garbage, and the like. Plus, my physical exam last month was a real shocker. In addition to the bad news on my weight, for the first time in my life I was told that my blood pressure was too high. Taking on the pressures of that new administrative position probably played a role in spiking my blood pressure. Why did I take that new job? I'd promised myself I'd never again take on an extra job, but I guess I fell for the combination of guilt ("Notre Dame needs your...") and flattery ("Frankly, we can think of no one better able to..."). Vanity, thy name still is. . .

So what am I doing at 8:10 a.m., on January 9, 2000, staring at the elevators on the first floor of Hesburgh Library? I'm looking at a sign that proclaims "Elevators under repair. Please take stairs." I guess it makes sense to do repairs early in the morning when the students are away on Christmas break.

I launched into an internal argument, "Why did I become a psychologist (13th floor)? I knew I should have become an economist (2nd floor). Do I really need those books? Well, I'm certainly not walking back to Haggar Hall empty-handed. Ah heck!"

After two flights of stairs I was beginning to breathe hard. Midway through the fifth flight I was aware that I was sweating. About the eighth floor I noticed that I seemed to be the only person in the stairwell. I guess it was around the ninth floor when the pounding in my ears and chest started, so I deliberately slowed my pace. As the sign for the eleventh floor came into view, I felt tightness in my left arm and shoulder, I sat down on the steps and panicked when I thought, "I might be having a heart attack."

I could hardly catch my breath and the perspiration seemed to be flowing in buckets. The thought that Nancy and I never got around to drawing up our wills leapt into my mind. I tried to shout, "Somebody, help me. Somebody, get a doctor," but all I could manage through my gasps for breath was a hoarse whisper that no one could possibly hear. When I realized that I couldn't even yell for help, it scared me half to death. So that was a negative teleography. Here's a possibly true, future story with a positive spin.

"A Stitch in Time"

I figured my little limp would gradually go away as the incision from the hip replacement surgery healed. For a time, things did seem to get better. Then, gradually, the limp began to get worse. Perhaps titanium hips hurt a bit in cold weather, I rationalized, and so I tried to just wait it out.

By Easter, I was convinced that the worsening limp could not be due to the weather. "Maybe I've just been babying this leg," I seethed. So I tried to walk it out. Wrong move! When Greg, my sixth grade son, began to call me peg leg, my wife, Nancy, knew something must be done. Nancy gave me a lift for my right shoe that she got from a shoe store. In two weeks, most of the soreness in my back and hip had gone away, and my limp receded to where it had been six months earlier. That was good enough for me. I could live without an exercise program.

Finally, Nancy fixed me with a steely gaze and said, "What am I going to have to do to make you go to the doctor to get your leg fixed right?" I didn't even want to imagine an answer, so I dialed the number for the South Bend Orthopedic Surgery and Sports Medicine Clinic. Three days later I was dodging my surgeon's, "What took you so long to come in here," accusation. Sure enough, my right leg was 1/4 inch shorter than my left leg. A quick trip to Ernie's Pedorthic Center on the corner of Ironwood and State Road 23—the store that used to house Little Professor's Bookstore before Barnes & Noble and Borders came to town—and I was fitted for two lifts (one for use with sneakers, the other for dress shoes). I immediately had no limp at all. "Golly, these new-fangled inventions sure are great," I thought.

Within two weeks I was walking two to six miles per day, five to six days per week. Nancy and I walked around the golf course at Knollwood on weekends—it was a nice bonus to get all that additional time to talk with her. I told all my students at Notre Dame, "I'm willing to talk about anything—careers in psychology, healthy lifestyles, dissertation topics, you name it—as long as you walk with me as we talk. Finally, instead of taking my kids directly home from school at 3:30 p.m., we now go back to Notre Dame. John plays basketball on the first floor of the Rolfs Recreation Center while I walk around the track suspended above the courts. Greg sometimes plays basketball with John, but being younger, the Notre Dame students are a bit too tough for him. Fortunately, Greg's a world-class fencer. So he often passes on basketball and heads over to fencing practice at the JACC. As he puts it, "Dad, pick me up when you're ready to go home. I think I'll go skewer a sophomore."

Lest you think everything is perfect in my life, I have two confessions to make. First, while my weight is now down to 212 lbs—I just can't get it down to 200 lbs, which is where I'd like it to be. Second, while I'd really like to take up swimming, my goggles and swim trunks continue to sit on a chair in my office. But I guess I can live with that.

Postscript

Recall that the purpose of a teleography is <u>not</u> to accurately predict your future. Possibly true stories of your future are best viewed as tools that might help you to create a better future than might have occurred, had you not told that story. Sadly, there are no control groups for your life. You can never know how your life would have worked out had you taken "the road not taken."

Did you like my positive teleography ("A stitch in time") more than my negative teleography ("He who hesitates")? Immediately after finishing "He who hesitates," I called my surgeon to set up an appointment to check out my hip. My appointment is next Wednesday. Now, what kind of a smart-ass comeback can I think up to cut him when he says, "What took you so long to. . ."

Life at the Crossroads for One Professional Woman
Amy K. Heesacker

Dear Abby:

I have a problem and you are the only one who can help me. I knew since I was a little girl that I wanted to be a veterinarian, but I recently had a really bad experience. My cat Bunny just had two kittens, and all that howling and mess in my mom's shoe closet really freaked me out. I don't think I want to be a veterinarian anymore, but I want to pick the right job because it will effect my happiness for the rest of my life. I read your column every day so I know you'll know what to do.

Signed, 12 year old at a crossroads

The Decision

At the age of 13 I renounced my budding career as a veterinarian and declared to the world, which was primarily my family at that stage of my life, that I was going to be a psychologist. My notion of a psychologist's function came entirely from the "Mostly About People" section (i.e., page 3) of my small, hometown newspaper, *The Daily Record*. At that time my role model and hero was Abigail Van Buren. I believed that if I could learn the answers to everyone's problems, and if I could develop the ability to profess my knowledge with as much confidence and humor as Dear Abby, then my life would be fulfilling. At the age of 13 I had no idea that newspaper advice columns were not standard work sites for psychologists nor did I have any inkling that I would finish graduate school without learning the answers to everyone's problems and with significantly less confidence than I had at 13. I did, however, come to appreciate the true value of humor, an appreciation that might not have been realized without the somewhat humorless labors of graduate school.

In addition to an ability to laugh through the most difficult moments of life, I took away many other things from my doctoral program in psychology. Not the least of which is my husband, Ed. Ed and I met the first day of graduate school at a private, midwestern institution. The two of us were thrown into a whirlwind of fresh faces and old egos, frightening departmental meetings about

TERMINATION DEADLINES and rapid-fire statistics lectures. Ed caught my eye and my interest from the beginning. Although we came from divergent backgrounds on many levels (e.g., ethnic origin, home town region, our parents' marital status) our passions, values and goals were strikingly similar. Ed helped renew my child-like love of life while also providing the support I needed to make the leap into adulthood. That first semester we learned a lot about each other and ourselves as we attempted to appear as if we were not surprised or scared by the ominous process we had just begged to undertake.

Ed and I married during our third year of graduate school, and we thought we had already seen some of our toughest times. We had realized by the end of our first year that if we could make it through statistics class together we could make it through life together as well. If only life was as simple as hand calculating a Student t-Test. Some of the decisions we had to make in graduate school seemed very tough indeed. In addition to starting and maintaining a relationship during graduate school, while in the process of developing our adult interests and our professional identities, we both chose to end previous relationships and face the repercussions of those decisions. Some of the tough decisions in graduate school were somewhat less intense but no less significant to our lives at that time. For example, we decided that each of us would keep our own names when we married and deal with the consequences for our children later.

Unlike many of the decisions Ed and I discussed, debated and rethought early in our relationship, my faith in my decision to pursue a career in psychology never wavered. Okay, I take that back. During late night data entry sessions in the department's windowless, closet-like computer lab, I had opportunities to reflect on the seemingly carefree lives of my hometown friends and question how dummy coding variables related to my chosen mission in life. Although it had seemed predetermined and obvious to choose psychology as a profession at age 13, the choice seemed murkier in graduate school at 20-something.

As I was making my way through graduate school many of my friends from high school were living temporary lives as motel cleaners and hair boutique cashiers so that they could afford to take glamorous summer trips around the world and spend weekends at the beach. During those moments in the closet with a computer, it felt that most 20-somethings were discovering themselves or at least enjoying themselves overseas or in less career-driven occupations while I was trapped by a decision I had made a decade earlier. I found myself longing for a job waiting tables, and surprisingly I found other female graduate students who had experienced the same unusual desires. I often half-joked that after receiving my doctorate I planned to find a culinary institute and throw myself into another career choice altogether. Despite these momentary lapses in focus, my plan based on a decision made at the tender age of 13 was all falling into place. During my 20's I had conjured up a dream of perfection that seemed to be coming to life. With very few disruptions to the schedule, I found a meaningful career course, successfully maneuvered through the somewhat random process of graduate school selection, survived a host of new challenges that were being placed in my path on a regular basis, managed to steer clear of those looming termination deadlines, and even picked up a co-pilot along the way who supported my every move. Choosing to work with children and finding relevant practicum opportunities was just icing on the cake. My 20-Something-Self believed that I was headed straight for the perfect married life with the perfect partner, the perfect career with the perfect child-based clientele, and the perfect relocation with the perfect timing to bring my plan to fruition.

> *Dear Abby,*
> *I have a problem and I thought you might be able to help. My husband and I have families in two different areas of the country, the northwestern most northwest and southeastern most southeast. We are in the process of making a lifelong decision and commitment that will determine our eternal happiness and the eventual well-being of our children's children: where to take our first jobs after graduate school. So please do not delay with your advice.*
> *Sincerely, 20-something at a crossroads*

What Happened?

The thought of two psychologists in a romantic partnership with one another conjures up enough amusing scenarios to support several seasons of a Thursday night sitcom. Although I could supply a network writing team with a humorous range of fertile material, it turns out that our new professional situation could at times provide the backdrop for a television drama series as well. My first indication that this would not be an entirely comedic experience was when the negotiations began for internship. In our graduate program a year-long internship is required, consisting of a full-time clinical position in one of many accredited professional facilities across the United States and Canada. As it became apparent that Ed and I would be seeking internship sites during the same year, we began to formulate the all-important question: What would we do if we were offered internships in different cities? The demand for a limited number of required internship sites by an ever-growing number of graduate students in psychology had created a frightening degree of competitiveness and a backlog of non-placed intern-wannabe's. Therefore, the possibility that we would not get an internship site in the same city was nearly inevitable, and the possibility that we might not get another chance at a first-rate internship in the future was a potential reality.

After surviving so much of graduate school together and after many heart-felt discussions, Ed and I decided that our first priority above all others (including completing graduate school if it had come to that, I suppose) was to stay together. Therefore the answer to the question seemed clear, or did it? If I get an offer from internship site in City A and you get an offer from internship site in City B and we have no other offers on the table, who's internship year will take priority? Previously hidden issues of gender equity began to emerge as internship selection day quickly approached and the all-important question became more relevant. Will it come down to a question of who was placed with their best fit (who gets their first choice) or will it come down to who should (deserves to?) go on internship this year? Should Ed get to go first because he remained in graduate school an extra year so that we could be together while I collected my dissertation data? Should I get to go first because I was coming from a non-traditional specialty program that seemed less well received by the internship sites?

Thankfully our first major crisis as a dual-professional couple passed with little fanfare. We beat the odds and managed to secure internship positions in the same midwestern city. Ed took a position at a university counseling center, and I worked in a large community mental health center. However, this very intense three-month period as we applied for, interviewed for, and waited for internship offers foreshadowed battles, struggles and heart-felt discussions about similar issues. Job searches, relocation, home buying, family-of-origin obligations, child bearing and rearing, and household chores are all topics of in-depth analysis in our relationship. I believe that for a woman at the beginning of the 21st century, these typical dual-professional couple issues are made even more difficult to solve by our precarious position between the freedoms and responsibilities of feminism. My understanding of feminism early in our marriage required that I confront any signs that I might be taken for granted or that I might not be respected for my contribution to the relationship. Because I had carefully chosen the perfect partner, I rarely felt that my rights or dreams were being thwarted. Quite to the contrary, I felt thoroughly supported, challenged and valued. However, when push came to shove I was not entirely certain that my best interests would be met. Would we get jobs in different cities and subsequently face a delayed and more difficult version of the internship dilemma? Would our jobs take us closer to my family in the north or his family in the south, and whose family would take priority? When would we ever decide to have children, and which one of us would give up their career to care for them? This was well-covered territory in our relationship, but problem solving always seems easier in the abstract.

When Ed told me he was offered a job in Florida, at the very same university center that he had reluctantly declined for internship in order to accommodate our decision to stay together, I experienced so many emotions at once that I wasn't sure what to say. Part of me was exhilarated about all the possibilities of relocating to a new region of the country. My mind's eye visualized lunches at small cafés surrounded by palm trees dreamily swaying in the breeze, early morning walks on white sandy beaches and of course weekly excursions to Disney World. However, a clumsy, unformed, and frightened part of me was crawling into my conscious mind and shouting warnings to me about disruptions to the plan.

"What about *your* perfect career plan to obtain the perfect job working with the perfect child-based clientele?" my developing, approaching 30-Self would demand.

"Hush now," my Youthful 20-Something-Self would answer, "This will be exciting and adventurous. You will find something wonderful in Florida. Don't worry, it's perfect!"

Despite my attempts to use the enthusiasm of my Youthful 20-Something-Self to quiet the whining of my Approaching 30-Self, it was becoming painfully obvious to both parts of me that I would soon become a "Trailing Spouse." What happened to the plan based on that decision made long ago? Had all those laborious pains of graduate school resulted in the delivery of an "M.R.S." degree? What if I could not find a job or worse yet, what if I could not find the perfect job? What did it say about me that we were going to pursue Ed's perfect job instead of mine? What did it say about me that I was so willing to follow my partner's career path away from my family and toward his? What did it say about me if I veered, for a time, from my own path?

In the end, the Youthful 20-Something part of me was successful in temporarily hushing the persistent questioning of the Approaching 30 part of me and I agreed to follow Ed's lead. We made the three-day drive from Michigan to Florida and Ed began his university job the day after we arrived. That left me at home to make unanswered calls to countless counseling facilities and wait dejectedly for our truckload of belongings to catch up with us. I started considering alternative options. Should I go back to school? Should I have a child? Should I demand that we move to the job of my choosing? I had approximately eight hours per day to think about how the decision I had made had compromised my plan and how my plan had compromised my life.

Facing 30, I began to look at how my decision at 13 may have stunted my growth toward culinary excellence or perhaps anthropological discoveries. As Lauren Docket and Kristen Beck write in their book *Facing Thirty*, at this stage of life "choices that had once seemed certain and solid may now seem to have been made of flimsier materials; a makeshift construction, erected to help us decide who we are (p. 46)." I look back on this time as if it was a particularly upsetting clothing crisis, frantically throwing off possible job role outfits that did not seem to fit me anymore and grieving over the possible career suits I had failed to take home from the store. Why had I chosen psychology? Just as I had briefly reflected on in graduate school, I began to thoroughly question the sanity of a woman who never allowed herself to explore other career options. Why was I so scared? What had I given up? What had I missed out on? I felt panic. Had I made the right decision? And right or wrong, would I have to live with this decision for the rest of my life? I felt overwhelmed and cognitively paralyzed. Suddenly it seemed that I was not in control of my life anymore. Graduate school was not easy, but at least the parameters were clear and I had over 20 years of practice at academics under my belt.

After a couple months of bearing the true ambivalence of my 20 years of decision-making or lack thereof, crying buckets of tears and sitting poolside in the Florida sun, I did find a job working with children. However, in order to supplement the meager income that accompanied my pursuit of perfection, I also took on a position evaluating sexually violent predators in the Florida State Prison system.

This was an exceptional decision on my part because not only was this position outside of the constraints of my plan, but I thought at the time that it might be outside of my capacity as a human being. Over the Christmas holidays in 1998 I accompanied my colleague, an expert in sex offenders, to the first civil commitment evaluation in the state of Florida. The interview closely preceded the enforcement of a new law designed to keep sexually violent predators from being released into the community before they have been rehabilitated. On that sunny holiday weekend, I sat in a tiny prison interview room (not unlike my graduate program's computer lab) safely across the three-foot table from the subject of our inquiry. My job at that time was to review the individual's prison record to corroborate or dispute the statements that were being taken in the interview. Upon opening the record I caught a glimpse of the inmate's birth date which caught my eye immediately because it was the same as mine. I listened as he described his lengthy history of abuse and instability, jail time, treatment courses, and prison transfers. I slowly realized that while I was struggling with the fear, disappointments and dream disruptions that are common to women facing 30, this man was facing 30 years or more of additional incarceration at the same point in his life. It certainly put my melancholia into perspective.

As one year became two years and two years became three years and as my shared 30th birthday with the inmate came and went, my melancholia slowly changed into productive reflection and insight that only comes with maturity. I began to realize that turning thirty did not mean the end of my life just as my last decision did not constitute the direction of the rest of my life. A man once told me that as you get older you make decision after decision and choice after choice until you have narrowed your path to a limited number of available options. At that time my innocent Just-Turned-20-Self unknowingly and angrily disagreed with that assertion, and later my 30-Something-Self knowingly and happily disagreed with that assertion once more. Fortunately that man was wrong in his prediction of my life and I was right to disagree with his negativistic view of human free will. As I began to smile again with satisfaction at my newfound appreciation for flexible life plans, I reflected on the women in my life that served as advisors and role models for me at this particular crossroads.

Dear Abby:
As a woman you will understand that it just helps to write to
you from time to time. It helps me even though I know you
don't know any more about the solution to my problem than I
do. I've got a lot to figure out right now: what to take as my
next job; when to have kids; and where to settle down. I can't
figure it all out today because, as you know, the plan is still
evolving. Write back if you have the time.
                    Sincerely, 30-something at a crossroads

Advice From the Real Women in My Life
        My mother is a quiet feminist, although I doubt she would
claim that title. Mom went back to school and worked outside the
home after my sister and I were safely enrolled in elementary school.
She reached adulthood during a time when a woman got married and
had babies, in that order, and then had the luxury to begin introspecting
about who she was and what else she might want out of life. Oh yes,
my mother had loads of time to spend introspecting about her
aspirations and self-development. When she wasn't goal setting or
self-actualizing, Mom was also feeding us well-balanced dinners,
keeping the house squeaky clean, ironing my Dad's shirts, actively
participating in every charity and women's group available in our small
community, sewing our Halloween costumes, accompanying Dad to his
work functions, baking cupcakes for our classroom birthday parties,
dreaming up creative activities to keep us from getting bored, and
occasionally sleeping. However, I cannot personally verify that she
slept.
        From my perspective, feminism in my mother's generation
meant having the opportunity and support from the community to seek
an education and work outside the home while still living as a woman
of the 50's the other 128 hours of the week. As two authors from my
generation wrote in their book *Facing Thirty*, "Even if our moms did
accomplish everything they wanted, they often did so *after* having kids.
Our generation, however, has come to the perplexing conclusion that
we need to get everything done *before* we start a family (p. 108)."
Although I still find the decision about when to have children
perplexing, what I learned from my mother is that life did not end after
she had two children in school and was facing 29. In my early years
she taught me how to read so I would be prepared for school and
reinforced my hard work when I got to school. Then when I got older,

she returned to school and modeled for me the importance of creating a path to your dreams even with major disruptions to the plan.

After leaving home for college to make my first independent steps toward my plan, my friend Honora provided my model of a graduate student and inspired me to continue toward my doctorate. Although to this day I wonder that all the frustration, long hours, and tears could have resulted in inspiration. Over the course of my four semesters of "undergraduate research experience," I closely observed in amazement and horror as Honora labored through a dissertation and the birth of her first child. I saw her struggle to maintain her professionalism in research meetings despite overwhelming nausea in her first trimester. I watched as she battled with herself over her desire to stay at home with her baby girl instead of rushing back to operate the lab. I listened as she negotiated the pros and cons of giving her baby girl a hyphenated last name versus opting to give her own last name as a middle name. I observed as Honora's length of time in the program extended past deadlines her male advisor had helped her establish. And I marveled as she persisted with her achievements while refusing to give up all that she was and wanted as a woman.

I soon found that Honora and I had a similar deficit with regard to discipline in the face of fruitful female conversation. We discussed the pros and cons of graduate school, the pros and cons of having children during graduate school, the difficulties involved with an advisor/advisee relationship, and how to make a really good batch of humus. One or both of us would often sigh at some point during the day and mutter, "Well, I guess we ought to get back to work." What I learned from Honora is that it is this type of woman-to-woman conversational bonding for the sake of bonding and relating and empathizing that creates meaning in the lives of women, or at least this woman. Although I have often struggled with my guilt over conversations that ran over self-imposed deadlines and discussions that replaced valuable paperwork time, I now question if these decadent detours were not the real work while the tasks were primarily distractions. As Gilligan notes in her book *In a Different Voice*, one of women's greatest strengths is that we value connections with others over individual achievements.

Connections with other women facing similar crossroads to mine are what ultimately helped me through that tough time of self-analysis after graduate school. I have leaned heavily on my best friend, Laura, from graduate school and the psychologist colleagues I have met since graduation, Anne, Janice, and Michelle. Each of my female confidants is a planner much like myself so they understand the discouraging nature of being a professional woman with a plan. However, because they have also recognized the value of talking, listening, and laughing our way through the tough times, they have supplied enough encouragement to help me push my way out of the cement suit I still occasionally choose for myself.

I talked with my friends about my ideas for this chapter before I started writing. They all agreed that ours is a shared struggle that could benefit from some written discourse. We have each been facing the same how-do-I-do-this questions about bringing our early plans to fruition, and I doubt that we are alone. How do we manage an intimate partnership while preserving our independent career goals? How will our career decisions and prospects be shaped by our decisions to become mothers one day? Once we decide that our early plans are not set in cement, how do we get past the immobilizing fear that makes change to the plan so difficult? I have been continually reminded that finding the support of other women in similar situations is more important than finding the "perfect" answer to any of the hundred of questions I pose to myself as I stand at the crossroads.

Supported by confident female role models and my patient, nurturing partner, Ed, I find myself surprisingly relaxed with my ever-fluctuating life plan. I chose to continue my work evaluating sex offenders and remained in Florida awhile longer than I imagined. Like clothes I might have picked out of the "imperfect" bin at the outlet mall, my 30-something life is currently fitting well enough to make me happy about the deal I got. However, more and more I am finding that my plan is not an outfit I have to squeeze myself into, but rather one I have tailored to fit my changing needs and desires. I am creating the meaning in my day to day life rather than hoping that I have chosen the life that has meaning.

I recently attended a conference for professionals who work in the sex offender field (ironically it was held at the Disney World resort). One afternoon on a break from the day's plenary session, I sat in the shade eating my lunch and watching the children playing in a typical Disney-style dancing water fountain. The strong shift in emotions and images from one setting to the other required that I take a moment to create some meaning in the situation. I have become a problem-solver who can share my knowledge of psychological concepts and human behavior in a way that helps people and hopefully makes the world a better and safer place for us all to develop. I can usually do that with some confidence and I am learning how to get fulfillment from what I do. Another man, my father, once advised me that I should not worry so much about making the wrong decision because after you make a choice you work hard to get what you need from the situation. He told me that when I looked back at my decision, I would discover it was the right one because I made it so. Looking back, he was right.

> *Dear Abby:*
> *From one professional advice giver to another, don't you ever wish you could just download the wisdom that comes with maturity into the pained hearts and minds of those who look to you for assistance? Life would be so much easier if we started out farther down the path, but then again would life be life without the tough stuff? Don't bother to answer.*
> *Sincerely, 40-something at the head of her path*

El Otro Lado
Mary A. Fukuyama

Let me introduce myself, as I begin to share my adventures encountered during a leave of absence from my position as psychologist at the University of Florida Counseling Center. Much of my professional life had been defined as a counseling psychologist, as a supervisor and trainer of counselors and psychologists, and as a counselor educator specializing in the area of multicultural counseling. I more or less had done all of the "right things" professionally, yet I was feeling disenchanted with my work life. After sixteen years in the field, I felt burned out and I was ready for a break. I was intrigued with the notion of a mid-career shift for self-renewal. And as a self-avowed multiculturalist, I was curious to know what it would be like "to practice what I preach" by entering into a cross-cultural immersion experience.

Fortunately, I was able to travel with my partner, Jackie, mostly through her encouragement and desire to do health care in Latin America. As a trailing spouse, I had the luxury of free time to write, observe cultural processes, learn Spanish, and engage in various work and leisure activities. This chapter is a compilation of email messages, which I sent home to my friends and colleagues, and the stories herein provide a personal narrative of our experiences in Guatemala. In these writings I contemplate themes of poverty and wealth and the implications of economic privilege. I also discovered the realities of cultural immersion which were both challenging and rewarding, and eminently much more difficult than I could have imagined.

I have titled this chapter *"el otro lado*," which literally means "the other side" in Spanish. I learned this phrase when I lived on the Rio Dulce River in Guatemala at a volunteer project site. Frequently we would go to *el otro lado*, the other side of the river. It became an expression for experiencing the position of "the other," which also affords views of a more known or familiar side of the river. This remotely located project site provided a metaphor for negotiating cultural differences and underscored the importance of being able to travel to the other side and to return home again.

What follows is a chronology of highlights from my electronic journal:

September 12, 1998,
Subject: First Impressions
We are located on the *Rio Dulce* River, which is a tourist attraction in Guatemala, near the eastern seacoast. We are one-half hour by motorboat to Livingston, a Garifuna community that feels like Jamaica. It's a treat to go into town by boat, a gorgeous ride through limestone cliffs draped lushly with vines and trees. Dolphins have been sighted in the river, which empties into the Caribbean.

This area is the home for over 6,000 *Q'ed-chi* (Mayans), who live in *aldeas* (villages) scattered throughout the jungles. It is also a vacationland for the wealthy, sail boaters, and *turista's* (tourists). The wealthy play here and the poor eke out a subsistence living. The land here is rocky and steep. It feels like Florida except more humid and green, and definitely not flat. There is a hot sulfur spring about a quarter mile up river, and a cool water tributary down river a bit. In the area there are *fincas* (farms) for cattle and fruit. Equitable land distribution is still a problem here. I think being here is a lesson on classism and social justice on the most basic (human rights) level.

The project we are working with has a clinic that is a primary urgent care center, a school, an agricultural project, and a papermaking project. I'm working with the papermaking project (hand made paper products), which the Mayan women make as an income-generating project. I work in a small shop that is located right at the dock. I see people come and go and I catch the afternoon breezes. My partner, Jackie, is here to do midwifery training with the Mayan women. Did I say it was hot and humid here? The humidity is ten times as bad as Florida in the summer, although the river and afternoon breezes mediate it some.

A typical day starts at about sunrise 5:30 or 6:00 AM. Because it is so hot, many people do their laundry early in the morning, washing it by hand in the river. It hurts my eco-consciousness to see the river used for everything, but that is life here. Work starts around 7:30 AM and goes 'til 4 or 4:30 PM with a break for lunch, the main meal of the day--soups or other main dishes, beans and rice and tortillas at every meal. For example, today's lunch was beans and rice cooked with coconut milk, cabbage-beet salad, and potatoes cooked in a tomato-based broth, spiced up with a fresh *picante* sauce. The food is fresh but the weekly menu lacks variety. There are chickens pecking around the dining hall, a mother hen and chicks and a prominent black and white speckled rooster. Today when I looked at the scraggly chickens clucking about, I saw only meat walking around. I saw my first case of malnutrition the other day--not a pretty sight. The 2 1/2-year-old boy didn't look like he was going to make it. Most health problems here involve either machete wounds or dysentery of some kind, and malaria, too. I look forward to visiting a village soon. It takes a boat ride and a hike uphill to get to them.

Life revolves around the river. It is probably about two football fields across in width. There is a view from the shop of the coastal mountains across the water, and thatched roofs accent the shoreline of *el otro lado*. Tonight we canoed across in our *cayuco* for dinner at a family run restaurant: shrimp and fried fish and cold drinks. I am learning to appreciate simple treats, like fresh ginger cookies and coconut bread purchased in town. The heat and humidity here is oppressive, but the best way to deal with it is to jump in the river and swim.

September 18, 1998
Subject: Here is the scene

It's about 7 PM at night and it is pitch black. No city lights. The night sky is clear and the Milky Way makes a bright swath across the heavens. The generator is humming in the background and provides electricity to the clinic, but I am writing on my new laptop by candlelight in our little house. The ebb and flow chirping of crickets and cicadas are in the surrounding jungles. We live in a two- story *casita* about 14 x 20 feet and the roof is constructed of palm leaves. It is open air; we sleep under mosquito netting. There is enough room for a hammock and a one-person size desk and chair upstairs. I have a battery run five-inch tall fan blowing on my face. Champa incense helps to ease the musty odor of mold caused by the intense humidity. Frogs begin to bark. I hear music in the background that sounds like a polka band; it's from an evangelical church across the river.

This past week was Independence Day (September 15) and lots of rich *Guatemaltecos* came to the river for a vacation. The bad part of that for us was their large motorboats, obnoxiously noisy, created huge waves that were dangerous for *cayucos* and knocked our boats about in dock. It seemed like an obvious metaphor about excessive power and obliviousness on their part.

Being a "volunteer" is a rather odd role, I think, but I am mostly just trying to take it all in. I am thankful to have been here for almost two weeks without getting sick. I am learning how to be more in the moment. Planning is not a big thing here. The usual speed is more gradual. It's like "people may get things done but we don't know when exactly. But things do happen; just don't get in a hurry over it." I'm not trying to be sarcastic, but the life here is much more circular (or organic) than linear (and direct). For example, getting people on the boat to leave for anywhere looks like this: what time does the boat leave? Oh around 1 PM. So at 1 PM the *gringa* (that's me) shows up but no one else does. Gradually people who are going on the trip arrive and leave and arrive again. Finally, the boat driver gets in the boat and whistles or otherwise announces that he is ready to leave (based upon the collective mass of people waiting). There are always a few stragglers who have to hurry to jump on. The bigger the group, the more elongated the process. Things here definitely do not work on clock time (except that the express busses between cities run on clock time). I tried three different trips into town to get something photocopied for Jackie, but each time the machine was broken. Then today I found a different store with a machine that worked. Yea!

It is different for me to experience cultural differences rather than to read about them. I note the contrast between the value of directness and getting things done versus circular discussion and hanging out as a way of doing things. This is, of course, complicated by the fact that I have a limited understanding of Spanish and no understanding of Q'ed-chi language and customs. The best thing about being here is the beauty of nature and the friendly people--the worst so far is the humidity and outhouses. This experience makes me think about materialism - its limits and seductiveness.

For tonight, tiny bugs flit around my lighted screen as I sit under the mosquito netting and rest on my bed...a safe haven from the intensity of learning Spanish and hiking around (our house is a good "Stairmaster workout" from the main buildings).

Well there are lots of observations to be made about this little spot on the planet. So far it is interesting, but I am also aware that I miss friends from home and the conveniences that I take for granted, like refrigeration and laundry facilities, flush toilets, garbage pick-up, whole wheat bread, mail service, streets, air conditioning, and lights in the house at night.
September 25, 1998
Subject: Tensions Rise

I've been here for three weeks to the day. My adjustment process is going along ok. I am moving beyond physical adjustment and now entering into the realm of emotional adjustment! I am bemused that I just read a book on cultural adjustment and now expect myself to be able to follow the author's advice. My latest issue revolves around my "worker role" in the papermaking project. Although I am in a cushy location in a small workshop and sales area right on the water, I am working with a young woman who has to keep her young children with her all day. They are ages 4 and 2 and they are just normal kids. However, after a few hours we all get tired of each other and they get fussy and their mom either scolds them or hits them or both, depending on the grievance. I lost my temper with all of them yesterday afternoon. I don't really have to be in the shop all day and so now I see the wisdom of my taking breaks.

Some of my frustrations are related to communicating in Spanish, the second language for all involved. Since I am still a beginner, I require a lot of patience with myself. I had three weeks of language school in Qetzaltenango last June and I am taking language lessons with an engaging Argentinean woman who lives down river a bit. The heat is hard on me, although it cools down when it rains, especially in the evenings. The constant heat and sweating is tiring.

The river is like a highway and the motorboats are the equivalent of cars. Having power means you have access to transportation. I feel a bit more empathy for kids who want to borrow the family car (read boat).

All of this feels like a lesson in appreciation of things that we have or don't have: For the little things in life which make it beautiful and enjoyable, like sunsets on the water, the gentle swing of the hammock, afternoon breezes, little yellow breasted birds, and taste treats like cream cheese on crackers. Some days, taking a cold shower actually feels good.

October 6, 1998
Subject: Today I caught a ride down river

Today I caught a ride down river with a tourist boat to the *Casa Rosada*, a project friendly hotel in Livingston where we eat good food and chat with tourists. The owner is a woman named Kathy from California and she is running both a business and social service here. Anyway, it is a change in scenery and a break away from the "rock," as we affectionately call the project site.

We live one day at a time by necessity. The term *"mañana"* seems to mean that anything that doesn't get done today can get done tomorrow. Do you think the university would accept that perspective? I get to think a lot about the way we create relationships with material possessions and money and the use of the same for ego gratification or entertainment. One of the contrasts here is that gasoline is expensive and necessary for survival (transportation up and down the river). Yet we see expensive powerboats pass by and they are using the gas just for entertainment. An ambience of "scarcity mentality" and limited resources pervade the area, and the skinny scab-ridden dogs personify the lack of physical nurturance. What do I mean by scarcity mentality: the psychological stress related to limited resources, which manifests in survival tactics, hoarding, petty theft, resentments and jealousy, control struggles over use of the motorboats, anger against the rich, stoicism, and always feeling as if there is "never enough."

October 10, 1998

Subject: More Frustrations

I have entered Stage II of cultural/country adjustment, that is, I am less entranced by the exotic and different and more distressed by the differences and adjustments. I reached a peak of frustration related to my work situation. The most upsetting part of working with children in the shop is when their mother gets short tempered and punishes them either with her strident voice or by slapping them. That bothers me more than anything. I think about how if this situation were happening in the USA, by law I would have to report her to the Child Protective Service. Although the two-year old is a fairly charming child, he is a toddler, and frequently walks off to explore, which triggers my vigilance. When the 4-year-old is also in the shop, they are fine when they play and entertain each other, which lasts all of about 10 minutes. I "stress out" when they fight. Regardless, part of my "job" is hanging out with the kids, and as I *accept* this fact, it makes life easier.

The other thing I needed to do was clarify my "job expectations" for myself and with my co-worker in the shop. I asked for help from another volunteer in translating to Spanish. I decided that I would work half-days, mostly mornings in the shop, and do other jobs in the afternoon, like write or help out with handy-person jobs. I think limiting myself to part-time will relieve a lot of my tension. I don't mind the work of the shop, which involves decorating hand made paper products, and preparing them for market. That's actually kind of fun for me. The past two weekends I went to tourist sites upriver and marketed the products successfully to local businesses (two marinas and a tourist hotel). The people in the area are supportive of the project overall. I never thought I would be a traveling salesperson.

Part of the tensions in the workshop also relate to the fact that my predecessor was very active in organizing and running the shop and business and my co-worker was highly dependent upon her. I, on the other hand, am just learning the procedures. I have also been told that I am a transition person, and that my co-worker is being trained to take over more responsibility. That is a bit challenging for her as she has a 3rd grade education, and at this point, follows rules more than grasps the big picture.

However, this last weekend she decided to go with me to one of the marinas so she could see it and meet the manager. We spent the afternoon there; so I am confident she can return on her own to make a delivery when needed in the future. This past week was much improved between us, as a result of our consultation with help of a translator.

Now I understand better why *extranjeros* (foreigners) tend to gravitate to each other (for shared language) and try to replicate aspects of home culture for comfort sake. There are opportunities here to do that, with each other (there are about eight foreign volunteers here) and at tourist sites run by folks from the USA (Casa Rosada, Mario's Marina). I have to admit that the breakfast cinnamon bun and slice of pizza for lunch were treats when I visited Mario's yesterday. Actually, this is another story. On Saturday mornings they have a swap meet at the marina, which is like a collective yard sale for people who live on sailboats. I took a supply of handmade paper products (postcards, picture frames, etc) and sold them at one of the provided tables, like at a craft fair. I sat between a fellow who was swapping engine parts and selling used snorkeling gear for the price of a beer and a couple who were selling vanilla beans from Madagascar and cigars from Cuba. The whole event took place in the restaurant's bar, so by noon most people were tanked up on Bloody Marys and beer. It was a cocktail party. It made me wonder about the correlation between leisure lifestyle and alcohol consumption (boredom? lack of meaningful work?).

I was surprised by my symptoms of phase II: my temper and lack of patience. I pride myself at being usually cool and contained. Being here creates situations that have reduced me to my most basic level of survival needs. Here is a "critical incident." This past week my co-worker gave me a plantain from some she had been given from our project's organic garden. I took this as a sign of peace making between us. I held onto it all day, and decided to eat it for dinner. The dining hall is a free-for-all in the evenings; everyone is on his or her own to eat lunch leftovers or to cook their own food. I proceeded to slice and fry my plantain. One of the other workers came in and thought the plantain on the stove was part of her dinner similar to that which her roommate was preparing. She turned up the heat. When I proceeded to cook it, she approached me. I reacted as if she were saying it was hers. I was surprised at my "this is mine" kind of response. But actually she apologized because she had thought that it was her dinner. Then I felt embarrassed at my "selfishness" but maybe at some level I was also a bit desperate about getting a meal. Most of the time there is enough to go around, but I react with some self-protectiveness, and sometimes hoard things and sometimes share.

Because I am an introspective person, first I react at the situation and then I am embarrassed at my reaction. Jackie says I need to practice loving kindness on my reactions.

November 2, 1998

Subject: Day of the Dead

We have been traveling for almost two weeks. Most recently we visited the town of Chichicastenango. We went to "Chichi" in order to experience the Sunday market. We also imagined there to be some ceremonies or processionals because it was Halloween weekend, All Saint's Day, and Day of the Dead. We were not disappointed. In the afternoon we followed our ears and found a live marimba band, and next to it, a gathering of local indigenous people who were drinking an *atol* of corn, a warm tortilla soup with the consistency of mush. Men who were dressed in special outfits extended it to us as they passed gourd cups along a human chain. A couple of the shrines, which were to be transported in the morning, were in the street for close inspection. Saturday night could have been a sign of activities to come as buses or trucks arrived all night, and occasional fireworks (bombs) were exploded. Read into that statement a night of disrupted sleep.

On Sunday morning, all of the energies seemed to converge in the square, fully packed with vendors in stalls of plastic blue or black tarpaulins, needed due to the heavy rain that had begun to fall. A marimba band (sax, clarinet, drums) played and men dressed in sequined outfits danced the dance of the conquistador, wearing masks depicting the Spanish conquerors, playing gourd shakers, wearing bells on their shoes, headdresses of multicolored feathers, not unlike a Mardi Gras party. There were a few young boys also learning the dance. They danced endlessly. Then amidst many fire rockets, the procession began at the church steps. A brotherhood of men, dressed in dark heavy capes and short pants and colorful hair wraps were the assistants, and carried church sacraments like the cross and other symbols. Other men carried statues of the saints in casements on litters on their shoulders. The extra decorations made the statues appear to be about 15 feet tall, decorated with fruit, mirrors, and plastic flowers. The saints were dressed and had money pinned to their outfits, not unlike a nightclub act. The dancing conquistadors joined the parade, followed by a marimba band, yes, they carry the marimba and play it while walking down the street, and a large marimba is about 10 feet long. A cluster of indigenous women followed behind one of the shrines; some carried candles. This moving mass worked its way through the crowded market streets, a feat in itself. More fire rockets exploded in the middle of it all. It was chaotic and festive and colorful and scary all at the same time.

We decided to return to Guatemala City via tourist minibus, which was in itself a godsend because the public bus service had been reduced due to bad road conditions. We saw many landslides (*derumbes*) that had closed at least one lane of the road in various places. The country is in shut down mode, due to many road closings and also a bridge out between here and the project. We are lucky we left before the storm system hit (Hurricane Mitch).

So here we are, back in the city project office, awaiting our exit in the morning. We are re-thinking our work plan at the project site. Jackie is renegotiating her job expectations with the project director to separate the midwife program (an outreach and teaching effort) from the health clinic itself. Although Jackie had a positive experience taking the midwifery training into the villages, she is having a control struggle with the medical doctor who is in charge of the clinic. This person is another volunteer from the States who wants to run the midwifery program in her own way. We are disillusioned with aid work in general and disappointed with the lack of infrastructure at the project site. It is ironic that the project sponsored a conflict mediation workshop for the Q'ed-chi, but the volunteers can't seem to work out their differences. So we are in a period of re-evaluating what we are doing in Guatemala. It will be good to come home and to get some perspective on this experience.

November 10, 1998
Subject: Re-entry

Having been out of the USA for two months, it is interesting to see what new perceptions or awareness I note upon re-entry. Also, it seems time for reflection about my experiences to date. In the back of my mind I think about my book project with Todd Sevig and our premise that spiritual values assist the multicultural learning process, and vice versa. I asked Jackie what she thought about this, and she said that she meditated more in Guatemala than at home, especially when she was alone, and her spiritual practices helped her to cope. For me, when I was stressed out over some interpersonal situation, taking time to meditate was a reminder to return to the "heart" and to start afresh each day.

Re-entry point, the Atlanta Airport...technology nation, big spaces, follow the signs. This is a nation of such individualism. People travel alone. In Guatemala, the Q'ed-chi people would not think of going somewhere alone. Going through U.S. Customs, a golden retriever is in training to sniff out drugs. It successfully meets a test case by pointing out a woman traveler wearing a fanny pack planted with contraband. The customs agents are happy; the dog has only been in training for 6 months. Lots of security checks, my boots trip the metal detector. An automated announcement cautions travelers to maintain control of their bags at all times. A man walks by talking on a cell phone. Ben and Jerry's ice cream...our first indulgences come with hot fudge topping.

After one week back in Gainesville, and a week's rest from it all, I don't have regrets, but perhaps more questions than answers. It was definitely more difficult than I could have imagined. It was a continual process of adjustments from day to day and week to week. It has been a lesson in appreciation for much that I take for granted. And at some level, I am trying to understand the impact of economic inequities, privileges, and distribution of resources.

November 15, 1998

Subject: Reflections on Cultural Contrasts

Group vs. Individual: We were told that the Q'ed-chi indigenous culture is collective vs. individual. Certainly they are not encouraged to "stand-out" from the group, and gossip and jealousy are ways of expressing group pressure to conform. Women who attended Jackie's midwife training were concerned that they would not be believed nor trusted by their sister villagers. The Q'ed-chi do not value being alone, nor sleep alone. Families live together in one-room houses and sleep in hammocks or on floor mats, sometimes 20 people (plus animals, chickens, dogs, pigs). Once, when Jackie was in the village to do the training, she was momentarily alone and got ready to read a book. Out of concern for her, a young boy who could speak Spanish was sent to keep her company until the rest of the group returned from church services.

Value of Education: The Q'ed-chi Mayans are one of 22 Mayan language groups indigenous in Guatemala. They are subjected to discrimination and prejudice from *Ladino's* (Spanish dominant culture) and aware of 500 years of oppression since the Conquistadors. There are few opportunities for bilingual education. Boys are lucky to reach an educational level of sixth grade. Girls are not encouraged to go to school, but rather to master the skills of running a household.

Gender Roles: There is an overlay of *Ladino* patriarchal values and Q'ed-chi values. According to a Mayan consultant, male and female roles are complementary and respected. However, we heard that men beat their wives to keep them in line, and children are hit when disciplined. Men have to deal with the external world, business transactions, farming, while women are expected to maintain the home. However, women often were selling their wares in the marketplace and working next to their husbands in the fields. Many funding agencies from North America or Europe are interested in women's empowerment, but what does this mean for the indigenous women?

Religion: Current trends in Guatemala indicate a rise in Evangelical Protestant religions, a long history of Catholicism, and a mixture of indigenous customs among the Mayans. The Evangelical movement seems to have been supported politically, whereas Catholic priests were targets during the civil war years. There is also a Mayan religious revivalist movement. The indigenous cosmology is related to the earth and planting of corn, and shares with North American tribes the custom of "calling the four directions" as part of opening ceremonies. Catholicism has incorporated indigenous customs, while Protestants prohibit continuation of these practices.

Politics: Although a Peace Accord that settled 36 years of civil war was signed two years ago, the country is still in a state of shock and recovery. They are taking testimonies of victims to establish what happened during the war, but once these papers are translated into English, they will be sealed and filed (not open to public scrutiny) in the United Nations for the next 20 years. Many people do not believe that the war is over. The people in power are pretty much the same. There is a "code of silence" and people do not talk about the war. However, it is documented that the military used a "scorched earth" strategy and eliminated whole villages in order to intimidate the peasants as well as keep their resources from the guerillas. Now people live in fear of robbery and the wealthy have to protect themselves from kidnappings for ransom.

Economics: Unfortunately this is a country of extremes. The wealthy comprise about 10% of the population, 15% are poor, and 75% are extremely poor. The indigenous population is about 80%. Large plantations still dominate the country's agricultural system, leaving the poor land for the indigenous people to do subsistence farming. We could not get a good cup of coffee in Guatemala because good coffee beans are exported. The average salary was about $100 per month, and a teacher earned about $200 per month. On the other extreme, I read about a golf course in Guatemala City in the Delta Sky Magazine. The author noted that local (presumably wealthy) golfers have personal bodyguards and are asked to check them at the gate and pick them up on completion of their game.

We saw many trucks and container ships with the "Dole" brand on it. The large fruit and coffee plantations here still exploit the workers. It makes economic injustice look pretty mean. Big business interests have always seemed to influence the US's international foreign policy. Dole owned United Fruit Company was behind a US invasion in 1954 when there were stirrings of land reform. It makes me wonder if the American public cares enough about such issues when it might impact the price of coffee or bananas or pineapple, or gasoline as related to the Middle East.

December 31, 1998
Subject: Disappointment

We have struggled with a decision about returning to the project, and Jackie tried to negotiate with the director to have her program be separated from the health clinic administration. However, this was not acceptable to the *gringa* medical doctor in charge of the clinic, and the project director sided with her. Once again I am flabbergasted that an agency, which has so many staffing needs, doesn't have the infrastructure to deal with personnel conflict. While it is a disappointment for Jackie not to complete the project, which she set out to do, it is quite honestly, a relief for me not to return to the project site.

I think we were naive going into this project. We have learned that NGO's (non-governmental organizations) often have shaky reputations administratively. They are inspired by well-intentioned people, but are not necessarily accountable to their funders or well organized. We heard some horror stories about how grant monies were misused or manipulated in international aid work. In addition, there is an intrinsic imbalance of power between the "haves and have-nots" and it seems to us that aid work perpetuates racism and cultural imperialism. While it seems that it has been important for the international community to have a visible presence in countries where there is severe political oppression (such as Witness for Peace in

Nicaragua), the appropriateness of aid programs is another matter. While we saw some good coming from the project where we lived (educational opportunities and respectful health care for the indigenous Mayan people), there were also instances of culturally inappropriate but well-intentioned interventions. For instance, the presumption that technology from developed nations is superior to indigenous ways of knowing.

I learned a lot while we were there. I learned a lot about what I don't know. Americans live in relative isolation with respect to the world community. I gained awareness not only of another country and culture, but also got a clearer picture of myself as a person with economic privilege and power. I can't go to the grocery and buy bananas without remembering the Dole container ships and knowing that the plantation workers earn a pittance for hard labor.

August 15, 1999

Subject: Post-script

My experiences in Guatemala were influenced strongly by living in an impoverished area where the majority of indigenous people were living below poverty level. It was in these rather extreme conditions that I became aware of issues of privilege, entitlement, deprivation, denial, and shame associated with economic class. How did this get played out in Guatemala? By definition as *gringos* (foreigners), we were wealthy. We had lots of "things" like water bottles and jack knives and jungle cloth clothing. As tourists, we could travel back and forth and as far as the indigenous people were concerned, we had unlimited access to resources from *el norte* (the north). I grew up with values of sharing and generosity, and was taken aback by a scarcity mentality. But then, when I engaged in hoarding behavior myself, I felt shame. Sometimes I was reluctant to "indulge" myself in things, which I knew the others could never afford.

In reflecting upon these experiences, I am struck by the similarity of economic dynamics in Guatemala and the United States. In Guatemala, the disparities were just more obvious. If I had not left a middle class lifestyle for a period of time, I would not have the appreciation that I now have for the many resources and privileges that come with it. I am also struck by the pace of life in the United States, the preoccupation with work, busy-ness, and "doing" vs. "being" in the present moment. This fast pace applies to leisure as much as work. How much is "enough" in our consumer-oriented society?

As part of my adjustment process in returning to work, I have intentionally decided to work part-time. I am ever in search of balance between the internal and external worlds, and a four-day workweek feels just about right. Downsizing our lifestyle is not an easy task, but following the motto, "live simply that others may simply live," gives me encouragement.

What If Things are Getting Worse?
George S. Howard

Because the content of many classes can keep the real-life experiences of students at arms-length, faculty can easily lose touch with the day-to-day experiences of our students. After twenty years of teaching academically oriented courses, I found myself living in my own little Ivory Tower, located in the northeast corner of Notre Dame's large Ivory Tower. However, I recently began teaching a course in the "Psychology of Healthy Lifestyles," where students are required (among other tasks) to write their autobiographies and to actively take part in class discussions. Because of this class, some of he cracks in the walls of my tiny Ivory Tower are becoming larger and quite troubling.

Racism had been defeated, I told myself, back in the 1960's by King, Parks, Kennedy, Abernathy, Evers, and a host of other modern-day saints. It was reassuring to be able to look back on those "bad old days" and know that we had made enormous progress since then. On the surface, Notre Dame seems as racially harmonious as any other university. Despite the occasional ripple of racial tension that lapped against the base of my Ivory Tower, I placed my trust in the university's generally pacific surface. Real racism, I thought, had been buried almost thirty years ago.

Then I began reading students' autobiographical narratives. Themes of racial tension surfaced in about three-quarters of the papers. In almost one-fifth of the papers, ugly racism was a dominant motif. Our syllabus listed racism, along with sexism, homophobia, and religious bigotry, as examples of the sorts of unhealthy attitudes to be opposed in the course. In spite of this warning, several grade-conscious students wrote and argued in defense of their racist attitudes. Often the arguments were of the "they're more racist than us" sort, while many were justificatory ("Here are the things that happened to me that made me a racist"). What disturbed me most was the attitude of many that they were certainly not going to be the first to make a move toward improving race relationships. This avalanche of autobiographies and discussions has now completely dismantled my Pollyannaish assumption that things are getting better among the races. Space will allow only one example.

Since we need to protect his anonymity, let's call our protagonist John. From the start, John was different. One of only two minority group members in a class of twenty-two, he was the lone scowling face amid a sea of cheery smiles. At two hundred and forty-five pounds of what looked like chiseled granite, the word "football" leapt to my mind. John was a Notre Dame captain and linebacker.

The first day of class consisted of a free-ranging discussion of what psychology might offer to students' health and well being long after their college years were finished. Twenty-one students spoke at one time or another. You can guess who remained quiet and looked sullen throughout. I reminded all that one-third of each student's grade would be based solely upon my evaluation of the content of his or her comments in class.

Four students in class seemed reluctant to speak, so during the next two weeks I made a point of asking their opinions after interesting points had been made. All except John responded well to these invitations. John simply shook his head "no" whenever invited. I tried to accept his nonparticipation cheerfully.

By the third week I was very concerned because John still had not spoken in class. In a discussion of the nature of the "self," I pointed out that there is a voice in each person's head that furnishes a running commentary on what occurs in his or her life. I then asked each student, in turn, to say the thoughts of his or her "self" aloud. Every student was able to express her or his thoughts except John—who again simply shook his head. I was desperate to get John talking, so I insisted that he tell the class what the voice inside his head was saying. He glowered at me and said, "Don't say nothing!"

John came to see me after the class and suggested that we might meet for a few minutes before class each day. I was thrilled with his solution, and soon looked forward to our brief meetings. John was a willing talker in my office. He was current on all assignments and (to my surprise) he was enjoying the class immensely. John eventually managed to speak in class a few times that semester, but he remained by far the most reticent class member.

John's autobiography was an eye-opener. He admitted that his football prowess was the only reason he was at Notre Dame. His preparation for college had been woefully inadequate. He had to work twice as hard as other students just to maintain a C+ average, and he did so.

What really startled me in John's autobiography were the examples of racism that he endured at the hands of his Notre Dame classmates and dorm mates. The insults and abuse were reminiscent of what people experienced in Alabama and Mississippi in the 1960's. In one memorable scene, John returned from the library at 11:30 P.M. to find his three suitemates quite drunk. For no apparent reason, they leveled a barrage of insults and racial slurs at him. John wrote that he began to reply, and then told himself to, "Don't say nothing to them." He reported that he still doesn't know how he restrained himself from beating his drunken suitemates to a pulp. Wisely, he went directly to bed and tried (unsuccessfully) to sleep. John reported that fighting his suitemates would have resulted in his suspension from the football team, and could possibly have cost him his scholarship. I feel sorry for any offensive linemen he might have encountered in practice the next day.

I invite students in the "Psychology of Healthy Lifestyles" course to drop by my office to chat in subsequent semesters. While about 75% of the students take me up on this offer, neither of the two minority students from John's class did so. Upon occasion I saw both of them on campus between classes, and we had brief, pleasant chats. Thus, I thought little of their decision not to stop by my office. However, when I invited all graduating seniors that I had taught (and their families) to a graduation brunch, all majority group students either attended or called to report a conflict. None of the minority group students called or attended.

I would like to think that John and other minority group students at Notre Dame aren't avoiding me and/or their classmates. I hope that the racial tensions on all college campuses are not as bad as they are sometimes portrayed in the media. I also hope that real progress on race relations has been made over the past thirty years. But these hopes might be unfounded. Perhaps we are not making progress in reducing racial tensions. At times I even allow myself to ask a terribly troubling question, "What if things are actually getting worse?"

Different Directions
Edward A. Delgado-Romero

Steve was one of the most likeable people I have ever met. He was the all-American guy, a former college football player who still carried himself with the confidence of an athlete. Steve had a subversive sense of humor and a disregard for authority that I could relate to. He was a recreational therapist and was extremely popular and well liked among his co-workers and the patients at the mental health facility where we both worked. In time we formed a relationship that endured eight years, two cross-country relocations, and one divorce. For a short time Steve was one of my best friends. Steve was also one of the most vehement and hate-filled racists that I have ever met. I struggle to reconcile how both those things could have been true.

I didn't realize how racist he was at first. Although in retrospect it's hard to see how I could have missed it. Admitting to myself that Steve and his family were racist and deciding what my relationship would be with them was a difficult process that involved a lot of self-refection and turmoil. A lot of what happened between us was correlated with my own developing identity as a Latino. My parents were immigrants from the South American country of Colombia and as a first generation American I struggled with my ethnic identity. Initially I denied and was embarrassed about being Colombian, especially since people held negative stereotypical views of Colombians (e.g., coffee bean pickers or drug dealers). It was easier telling people that I was Spanish because then they thought of me as a White European. If I was Spanish, I was basically White like everyone else.

Steve and I both worked in a residential treatment center in Memphis, Tennessee where he was a recreation therapist and I was a counselor. After several months of working together, Steve invited me over to have dinner and meet his family. I was nervous about starting a new friendship because I had moved back to Memphis a year after graduating from college to be closer to my college friends. Things had not worked out as I planned. Instead of being surrounded by my fraternity "brothers," I felt isolated and betrayed by friends who seemed more interested in reliving our college days than developing our adult friendships. Consequently, I put a lot of pressure on myself to make new friends.

Steve and his family were very welcoming of me. His wife was friendly, and his stepson and I discovered a mutual love of video games. After introductions I was given the grand tour of their home. One corner of their home caught my attention: the corner of the living room which displayed various decorations, statues, dolls and advertisements featuring "negroes" with ink black skin, huge red lips, wide open eyes and big bushy afros. Many of the decorations alluded directly to slavery. The decorations were intended to resemble decorations from the old South, but these weren't antiques, everything was brand new. I had never seen things like this, despite having spent most of my life in the south (Georgia and Tennessee), seeing these decorations in a home caught me by surprise. I chose to overlook them. I thought surely it must have been a joke or some harmless Southern custom. The rest of the evening went well as long as I didn't look over in that corner.

Despite all his tough posturing, there was a sensitive side to Steve that he kept hidden. He had a sensitive side that came out in his relationship with his dog, which he pampered and treated like a child. Steve liked to care for stray animals and people - he chose to work professionally with abused children and the homeless. I felt I could relate to this caring for others as I was training to become a counselor. I thought there were caring qualities in Steve that I could sense and help him develop. However in focusing on his positive qualities I was willing to overlook Steve's negative qualities that slowly became more apparent. One of our main bonding activities was to watch football games. After we had been friends for a few months, Steve began to refer to the African American athletes as "niggers." Nigger was not a word that I had heard said out loud much in my life. In fact the only time (other than in movies or comedy routines) that I had ever heard someone called a nigger was when an African American teammate called me a nigger when I missed my assignment on a play during football practice. I stared at him and weakly answered "but I'm not black." He laughed at me and said I was a nigger not because I was black, but because I was stupid. Despite having attended a college that was 90% White in a city that was 60% African American I had never met anyone who was bold or stupid enough to say the word nigger out loud.

Intellectually I found it hard to understand why Steve would be calling people niggers given that we worked with African American co-workers and patients, and Steve never talked like this at work. In fact one of the people he spent the most time with at work, and seemed to genuinely like was African American! My first reaction was to laugh nervously, hoping he would stop. However, Steve took my laughter as a signal to continue, and his racist rants gradually became worse. I finally asked him to stop making the comments because I believed he was making them to bother me rather than because I though he believed them. Steve had a tendency to antagonize his friends and I saw this as another way for him to try to get under my skin. Steve took the hint and toned down his remarks - I thought that was progress, and my liberal conscious was allayed.

After two years of working together, Steve and his family left for Florida and I moved to Indiana to start graduate school. Soon after moving I decided to get a divorce from my first wife, and Steve was supportive when we would talk over the phone. He seemed to be doing well and enjoying a great deal of prosperity working for his father-in-law. Steve and his family came to visit me during a big football weekend. We caught up on old times and enjoyed a wonderful game. However, as the weekend wore on, Steve became belligerent with his remarks about African-Americans. There was a new intensity, boldness and venom behind the comments. Steve went so far as to make a very public comment in Chicago about an African American museum employee who wasn't moving fast enough for him. I hastily told him, "We're not in the South anymore, and black people will kill you for making those kinds of comments here." This was not a compelling reason for asking him to stop, and in fact it appealed to Steve's racist view that African-Americans were violent, but it served to quiet him down. I felt angry, scared, humiliated and embarrassed. Outside the museum I angrily confronted Steve again about the remarks and how inappropriate I thought he was being. Steve apologized for his behavior and promised not to make racist comments around me again. Specifically he agreed to refer to African Americans as "black people." As he boarded the plane back to Florida I was sure that I had gotten through to Steve, yet I was also relieved that he was leaving.

During graduate study in psychology I had a chance to work on my own ethnic identity. Graduate school was a challenging time in my life, I spent a lot of years working on my own issues at the same time I was being trained to help other people with their issues. During graduate school I learned about and reclaimed my Latino heritage. I took a trip to Colombia to better understand my parents and ancestors. I began to identify as Latino and felt idealistic about eliminating racism.

I assumed that because I had developed my ethnic identity and confronted racism, that everyone else would benefit from the same process, especially White people. I felt that I could help my friends, especially Steve, liberate themselves from the burden of racism. Surely with my help Steve would realize that he could not continue to be racist, especially if he already had one Latino friend. I couldn't have been more wrong or naïve.

I stopped by to visit Steve after interviewing at the University of Florida for a senior staff position in the counseling center. I had just finished an internship at Michigan State University that heavily emphasized multicultural work and had never felt better about myself either professionally or personally. I had good feelings about my interview and thought that there was a good chance that I would end up at Florida. One of the perks of living in Florida would be being close to Steve. We had talked about seeing each other on weekends and attending Jaguar football games in nearby Jacksonville. I was in a positive frame of mind when I drove up to Steve's new house.

Steve had moved from Jacksonville Beach to a small town about an hour inland. It looked like a typical small, southern town. Steve had room to raise his dogs and build a house. He was excited about the prospect of my relocating to Florida and that my interview had gone so well. We were both excited about watching the upcoming Jaguars playoff game. Things went well and there were no racist comments or racist decorations in view. I thought that perhaps Steve had some kind of epiphany, however during the game things began to fall apart. The Jaguars started to lose and Steve became angry with one of the African American players and referred to him as a "black person" as we had agreed to in Chicago. I felt some satisfaction that Steve had controlled his impulse to make a racist comment. That smug satisfaction did not last. Steve had also invited one of his new friends, a local guy, to watch the game with us. He looked at Steve with a puzzled look on his face and said, "*Black person?* Don't you mean nigger?"

Steve looked at me for one split second. Then he proceeded to let loose the most hateful, ignorant and deplorable racist rant I had ever heard. Steve vented his anger towards "niggers" and with each passing moment he grew angrier and angrier. If you had explained his behavior by telling me that Steve was possessed by a demon, it would have made more sense to me. I felt sick to my stomach as the veneer of our relationship was stripped away. Steve had been keeping himself in check around me, but now the hypocrisy and ugly truth were exposed.

Steve told me that the reason that I wasn't a racist was that I lived "up north," and he predicted that once I lived in Florida I would become racist as well. Steve told me that Florida was full of "niggers", "whiggers" (White "niggers"), "chiggers" (Chinese "niggers"), and "miggers" (Mexican "niggers"). Steve's stepson, once a cute kid with whom I played video games, was now a Marine who had trained under African American officers and served alongside Marines of all races. He echoed Steve's hatred for "all kinds of niggers". He told me this, without a hint of irony or insight as he stood in his bedroom where the images of Michael Jordan, Scotty Pippen and Shaquile O'Neal were plastered on the walls.

Steve told me that the only thing for White people to do was to move into all-White communities, like the one he lived in, where "no nigger would be caught dead after sundown" thanks to the local KKK. He also affirmed his devotion to his church and showed me a picture of a very Caucasian looking Jesus and the disciples. In a state of shock, my idealism gone, I made up an excuse and got into my rental car. I drove away and never spoke to Steve again.

In the time since my last interaction with Steve, I have had time to reflect and try to understand what happened between us. I don't know if I can ever understand the extent of the hate that seemed to consume Steve towards the end of our friendship. I can see that the hate grew and was magnified as Steve made choices for himself (such as moving into an all-White and racist enclave). But I don't know of any incident or negative experience that Steve had with African Americans that he didn't have with Whites. In fact, to the best of my knowledge, the people who had hurt Steve the worst were all White. In fact he had moved away to his enclave because his White father-in-law had fired and disowned him. Yet he didn't hate Whites.

Although it would be easy to focus on Steve's outrageous behavior, I was also to blame and guilty by association. My silent complicity in his racism and my continued relationship with him was the most confusing aspect of the problem. How could I, as a Latino, a counseling psychology graduate student and a multicultural activist have continued to have a relationship with a racist? Why did it take an angry, testosterone-and-beer fueled rant to make me see the truth? I wondered why I had continued to submit myself to that toxic environment - in essence becoming a second hand racist.

I realize that as my ethnic identity developed I became much better at identifying and confronting subtle and systemic racism because in educational settings that is what I faced. I also became bolder and more courageous in confronting racism in my life and among my friends and family. However the raw, brutal and elemental hatred that Steve revealed to me left me paralyzed. I just wanted to deny that it existed, I wanted to deny that Steve was really like that, and most of all I wanted deny that I had been his friend. Yet it was all true. Steve provided an encounter experience for me, one that stripped away all of the comforts, buzz words and jargon that I used to deny the problem of racism in my life. My experience with him inspired me to examine my beliefs, convictions and most of all my courage. Reading about the experiences of Holocaust survivors and about the life of Malcolm X helped me realize the need for me to strongly counteract even the slightest hint of racism and oppression in others and myself. Hoping for change and dreaming about a better future was not enough.

Steve and I went in different directions, both literally and figuratively, when we left Memphis. The seeds of who we were going to be had been planted long before we met, and meeting each other served to accelerate that growth. I don't understand the dark path he chose, and I'm sure he doesn't understand the path I have taken. While I chose not to keep in touch with Steve any longer, I do hope that he will eventually be able face his demons and liberate himself from the painful prison of racism.

I never asked Steve what he thought of my being a Colombian, because I knew the answer. Although he might say that I was an exception, I knew that sooner or later I (as well as my family or my children) would all be niggers in Steve's world.

On Being Tricked Into Attending College
Woodrow M. Parker

By the mid-1950's, more and more Black Americans in the South were beginning to attend college. In rural Alabama, where I was reared, the ways to improve your life were to either attend college, go north to find employment, or join the military services. The majority of young people left home to travel north in search of a better life or to enlist in military service. Only a few chose to attend college.

I never gave much thought to attending college. People who attended college, in my opinion, were middle-class, uppity people who lived on the south side of the creek (a small stream of water which was the dividing line in our Black community). I lived on the north side of the creek where the poorest people lived on small farms, in small shotgun houses, so called because one could shoot or see straight through the narrow structure if the front door and the back door were opened. Because children from these families were not expected to attend college, they were not encouraged to take the college preparatory classes or curriculum. Since placement tests were not conducted in those days, a student's ability was based on his or her socio-economic level or on where the student lived.

I attended the county training school for "colored" and was assigned classes in shop and vocational agriculture. I never took advanced mathematics, English, or science courses; and one might find it hard to believe, but throughout my twelve years of school, I was never given an assignment to write a single paragraph. I also never took a course in Algebra or Biology. Needless to say, I was not prepared to attend college.

I never saw myself as someone who would attend college. Most of the people in my family had never attended college either. In fact, the only college graduate in our family was an uncle who never talked about his collegiate experience. He had been in the military, where he served in World War II. Like many of the Black veterans, he attended Tuskegee or Alabama State Teachers College where he studied tailoring. My uncle was not a role model who would influence me to attend college. Although my parents valued education and encouraged me to reach for the stars where education was concerned, they both dropped out of school early and never had a college or university experience to share.

I had conflicting feelings about attending college. On the one hand, I did not want to spend my whole life picking cotton, picking up potatoes, cutting corn and loading watermelons. And I did not want to feel jealous of my cousins who attended college. Besides, I had heard some of the older Black people say that education turns a person into a "Fool." They also said that people who go to college think that they are better than people who don't go. Therefore, I had some feelings of resentment towards Black people from my community who attended college.

As a student in high school, I placed most of my emphasis on athletics and was not challenged to perform academically. There were several teachers who thought that I was college material, and they often talked to me about attending college. They "just knew" that I was a prototypical college student, but I did not see myself that way at all. I just had some different ideas and plans for my future. In particular, I thought that I would follow the lead of many people who lived in my hometown. After they became old enough, they most often would go to larger cities in the North, East or West. They migrated to Detroit, Chicago, Philadelphia, New York, and many other large cities to find jobs in factories, and anything they could find that would be better than the farm work in rural Alabama.

After working up north for several months, they would return home as models of success, driving expensive cars and wearing expensive clothes and jewelry, their symbols of success. In particular, the northern visitors would come home during the Christmas holidays or during the summer, and they would parade around town in their new cars, clothes and jewelry for everyone to see. Willie Lee Simmons had suits of every color in the rainbow, wore diamond rings on every finger of his hand, and drove a candy-apple red Ford Thunderbird. We local boys could hardly wait for Willie Lee to make his grand appearance. I thought this was much more exciting than going to college. My plan was to follow my older brother who had gone to Detroit and evidently made a great deal of money. I thought that I would graduate and go to Detroit and live with my aunt or my brother for awhile until I could find my own place and get a job in an auto factory and have immediate success and immediate gratification. Then I would return home to display my newfound wealth.

The return of African Americans to my hometown, showing off their cars and their clothes was a tradition that dates back as long as

I can remember and was a model for others to follow. Upon their return, these people would tell stories about how wonderful life was in Detroit, Chicago or New York. Not only were there great job opportunities, but there was life with no racial prejudice. It was just the opposite of all the hardship that we faced in our small rural Alabama town, characterized by such hard work as picking cotton, working in the potato fields and working in the corn fields. According to the stories, you would make more than one hundred dollars a day, and you could have all the wonderful things that a person could dream of. This sounded heavenly, because in Alabama, you were lucky to make more than five dollars a day.

So, not only could you make a great deal of money and have nice cars and clothes, but a person was treated with dignity and was treated as a human being, and there was no racism. White people treated black folks with respect, and you could go anywhere you wanted. You could live where you wanted, you could even eat in any restaurants you wanted, and it was not necessary for you to have to go the back of the bus, or to go to the back of the restaurant. You could go in and sit down among white people and eat a meal. You could even attend school with white people. I had never heard of this--attending school with white people. You could attend school and there was just no racism, according to the stories that they would tell. As I became aware of this world of magic in these northern, eastern or mid-western cities, I certainly did not want to go to college.

I would always present these arguments when my teacher would talk to me about going to college. He'd say, "McClain (my middle name), you ought to go on to college. I know Detroit sounds good, but it might not be all that they say it is." I had the proof, I mean, I had seen my brother, who had almost no clothes when he left home to go to Detroit, return with three or four suits, Stacey Adams shoes, Johnson Murphy shoes and Edwin Claps--all of the symbols of success. Not only did he have these nice clothes, but also he had bought himself what was known as a duce and a quarter--a Buick Electra 225. He came back with cars, suits, shoes and hats, and a pocket full of money, jewelry, and, surely, this was more attractive than going to college.

I had spent many days in the cotton field daydreaming about life in the large cities and how everything was just absolutely perfect. I would begin thinking about life in the large cities early in the morning as I began to work in the fields. I would often forget that I was in the fields, because I was dreaming about being in the city and returning to Atmore, my hometown, in the nicest car in which anybody had ever returned. What made the car so important was that growing up, there was never a car in my family. My father died when we were young, and my mother carried the total responsibility for our care. Of course, we worked to help ourselves as much as we could, but there was never a car in my family. A car became a symbol of success, and buying a car was even more important to me. Having gone through junior high school and now into senior high school, the moment had finally come for me to go to Detroit to find my fortune. One day during lunch hour, toward the end of my senior year, a young African American instructor, my senior advisor, called me aside and talked with me about my plans,

He said, "Parker, what are you going to do?"

I said, "I don't think you've been listening to me. I've been telling you for the last three years that I plan to go to Detroit and work in an auto factory. And I'm going to show you what I can do when I go up to Detroit, because I'll manage my money well, and I'll come back and show you that it's better to work in the factory than to go to college."

Then he answered, "Since you are so intent on going to Detroit to work, I'd like to make you a proposition. I'd like to buy your ticket to Detroit."

Now he had my attention. He wanted to buy my ticket to Detroit. This sounded really, really interesting because I did not have the money to buy my ticket. However, there was a catch. In order for him to buy my ticket, I had to first go to college for at least two weeks, and if I did not like it, then he would send me a ticket to go on to Detroit. Well, that seemed like a pretty good deal. I could go to college and pretend that I was interested in college for about two weeks. Then I'd give him a call and have him send my ticket. I'd get on the Trailways bus, and then off to Detroit I'd go.

If I attended college, I would encounter two major challenges. The first would be a lack of academic preparation, and the second would be a lack of financial support. Because I was no stranger to hard work and sacrifice, I could overcome the academic deficiencies. The greatest problem would be financial support. Although I explained this dilemma to my teacher, he told me to just give college a chance, and I should not worry about financial concerns. He had made a couple of calls to Stillman College to find whatever financial assistance he could get for me. I had never heard of Stillman College, but my advisor said, "Well, you know, Stillman College is a small college with a family-like atmosphere where you will fit nicely; and Stillman is on your route to Detroit." So I went on to Stillman College and was met at the bus station by a group of students who welcomed me and told me they had expected me to come. I was pleasantly surprised that this arrangement had been made, because this 200 mile Trailways bus ride was the farthest distance I had ever traveled from home. For these students to welcome me and take me to the dormitory and to my room was incredible. I went and met the person in charge of the dormitory who also seemed to me expecting me. He took me to my room, and some strange things began to happen to me immediately. I began to feel like I might belong in college.

Shortly after I arrived on campus, a small cadre of students met me and took me over to a social that was being held. I went to the social and met other students. I said to a few students, "Well, I'm just kind of passing through. I'm not really here to stay," but they would not hear of that. They just embraced me and made me feel as though I belonged; and I began to feel, almost immediately, that I had found my home. This was one of the strangest things that had ever happened to me in my entire life. After many years of rethinking those first few hours at Stillman College, I still do not fully understand the powerful dynamics that impacted me so severely.

Having spent most of my life planning to go to a city and find a job, I felt like my head was being turned around in a very strange way. I suddenly felt that I was where I belonged. It took me several weeks to figure out that I was not about to go anywhere else. I was going to stay at Stillman College! Within a few days, I found a job as a custodial worker in the women's dorm to help pay for tuition, room and board.

One day, when I was walking across campus, I ran into the Dean of Students. He said to me, "Well, Parker, how's it going?"

I replied, " Well, I'm doing okay."

Then he asked, "Well, did you find a job?"

And I said, "Yes I did."

Then he said, "What are you doing?"

I replied, **"I works in the women's dorm."**

The Dean quickly said, "Uh oh, wait a minute Parker. Remember that first person singular, present tense, has no 's' on the verb. So remember that now. You're not suppose to say 'I works.' If you graduate from Stillman College saying 'I works,' 'I teaches,' and so forth, you may never find a job, and you will be an embarrassment to your family, yourself and to Stillman College."

I realized in that instant that I needed to do something about my speech and about my understanding of the English language.

thought that maybe one way that I could improve my English--my speech and English usage--was to major in English. So I decided that I would major in English, and at least I would learn how to use the language more effectively than I did at that time. I would never be great at it, but at least I would be able to communicate. The other thing I decided was to take my time, and try and speak correctly, and that seemed to work out okay.

I still had a major problem, because the job as a janitor in the dormitory was not sufficient for meeting my financial needs. I had what was called a "C Work Scholarship," meaning that I needed to maintain a "C" average to keep this scholarship. With the scholarship, I could work and have enough money for my tuition, room and board, but I did not have enough money for such necessary things as clothes, toiletries, school supplies or anything else. My Mother, who worked in a laundry most of her life, could not help, because she had six children in the family and only made about sixteen dollars a week. Given this scenario, I needed to find someway to survive. I had decided no matter what, I was going to stick it out, rather than yielding to the temptation of leaving and going to the easy money in Detroit. Although I was poor and needed financial assistance, I was bound and determined to make it, because it seemed I had finally found my home.

Life is difficult on a college campus when you are poor. It is even more difficult when you are teased by fellow students for having so little. I was told I was so poor that I could bring all of my belongings in one sack. Someone suggested that I paid for my tuition with two pigs from my grandfather's farm. I was able to endure that joking and teasing because I had found the place where I belonged, and the thought of being a college graduate somehow became much more important to me than being able to return home in a nice car, fancy clothes and jewelry. The more they teased me, the more I became determined to "stay the course" until one day I became a college graduate.

By the time I thought I had exhausted all resources for securing additional money, something strange happened to me one Friday night that would positively influence the rest of my college life. I went over to the barber's house for a haircut, but the barber was so intoxicated that he could not cut my hair. When I attempted to leave, another customer came and sat in the barber's chair because he thought that I was the barber. Although I had never cut anybody's hair in my life, I thought, "Why not?" and commenced to cut the customer's hair. When I finished, he looked at his haircut in the mirror, nodded his head with approval, and paid me fifty cents for the job. In that moment, I thought of miracles about which my grandparents had talked and sung. This had to be the work of the almighty God, who empowered me with the confidence, faith and skills to cut hair, although I had never cut hair before. My grandparents gave biblical accounts of miracles such as Daniel being saved because God locked the jaws of lions in the lion's den; of God quenching fire in the fiery furnace to save the lives of three men; of David, a shepherd boy, killing the giant with a sling shot; and of Jesus feeding 5,000 people with a fish and one loaf of bread. Perhaps God had one more miracle left, and he gave it to me. Now I said as my grandparents would say often, "Blessed be the name of the Lord."

Before the customer left, he said, "Say, that's not a bad haircut. Thank you. I'd like to come back next Friday for another haircut." While I was excited and content with what I had done, I wasn't sure at the time that I could do it again. These feelings of self-doubt were shortly allayed, because my career as the campus barber took off by leaps and bounds. Fortunately, my barber back home gave me a pair of clippers and the other tools that I needed to get started, and the rest is history. I quickly became the college barber where I not only earned enough money to finance my college education, but also earned enough to help my mother and younger siblings back home. Every now and then, I run into people whose hair I cut while I was at Stillman College, and they introduce me to their friends and family as their college barber. Beginning with that day that I gave that miracle haircut to a stranger, I was never broke again. I always had a few dollars in my pocket.

For some reasons, people view their barbers as people in whom they can confide. My student customers discussed a wide range of problems and issues with me. I remember Eddie talking with me about his dilemma about participating in a city Bus Boycott that was planned to take place in Tuscaloosa, Alabama in 1962. Eddie was a tall handsome African American male from Eutaw, Alabama who was majoring in Biology. He had hopes of attending medical school after graduation. Because Eddie's grandparents had warned him against participating in civil rights activities, he was afraid to participate. His grandparents were afraid that civil rights activities would be a distraction from his schoolwork, so he was never to consider becoming involved. Eddie was the only child in their family to attend college and the first African American from his entire county to consider going to medical school. Eddie told me that he still wanted to participate because, as president of the Sophomore Class, he needed to show leadership. Additionally, Martin Luther King had suggested that each person in life needs to choose something for which he or she is willing to die. King suggested further that if you don't stand for something, you will fall for anything.

Eddie wanted to march desperately, but he did not want to go against the will of his grandparents. At some level, he agreed that his grandparents were correct. He knew several students from Alabama State University who had been dismissed from school for protesting. He really wanted to protest against bus segregation, but he did not want to be labeled a rabble-rouser who would later be denied admission to medical school. I don't remember if Eddie decided to protest or not. I do know that he realized his dream of becoming a medical doctor because I've heard that he is one of the leading pediatricians in Atlanta today.

Another customer to whom I spent a great deal of time listening was Sammie Lee Wells, who was considered to be a player or womanizer from Birmingham, Alabama. He enjoyed talking about women with whom he had sneaked on campus. Sammie would come for his haircut late Saturday afternoon because it usually took him all day to become sober from Friday night's binge drinking. There were times that his breath would smell so bad from the alcohol that I could hardly stand to cut his hair. He told me that he had been drinking alcohol since the ninth grade. According to Sammie, he and his buddies would drink wine after football games in the school's parking lot. When he first started drinking, it was a way to have fun and to feel good. However, after his eleventh grade year, he had formed a drinking habit and found himself needing more and more. When I asked him how his parents felt about his drinking problem, he said that they were too busy working and traveling all over the country to care. His father was a football coach who Sammie believed was disappointed in him because he was not interested in playing football.

Sammie did not seem to be interested in school either. Instead, he was mostly interested in chasing women and drinking. One day, I asked Sammie why he drank so much if it made him sick? He told me that he really did not know, but he always believed that he could stop drinking anytime he wanted.

Sammie told me that one night while he was drunk, Josh, a gay student came to his room and molested him. He seemed really upset and ashamed as he gave an account of Josh kissing and fondling him, but he said he was too intoxicated to defend himself. He asked my advice about whether he should report the incident to the dean. If he reported the homosexual encounter, Josh would be suspended immediately, because there was zero tolerance for gay and lesbian issues. I suggested that he attempt to settle the matter with Josh before going to the dean. I also offered to serve as the negotiator between Sammie and Josh. Fortunately, they worked through their differences and were able to work peacefully and in harmony. While Sammie worked through this ordeal okay, he was not able to work through his drinking problem. After finally graduating from Stillman, he had problems maintaining employment due to drinking. Recently, I received a call from a friend who told me that Sammie had died from alcohol poisoning.

In retrospect, I learned several lessons from this experience. First, when others see that you are putting forth a serious effort to help yourself, they are more likely to reach out to help you. James Brown, the King of the Blues, said it in the words of a song, "I don't want nobody to give me nothing. Open the door, I'll get it myself." In my case, I was given the opportunity to attend college, and I took advantage of opportunities to succeed with the support of a special high school teacher, coupled with a supportive college atmosphere which characterizes historically Black institutions like Stillman College. Seeing that I was trying to help myself, the barber back home gave me a pair of hair clippers, an essential tool for my trade. In addition, a professor observing that I was straining to see the blackboard, suggested that I take an eye exam, and later identified a source of financial aid to pay for eyeglasses.

Second, it is important to take risks and to be flexible. Going to college without having planned to go was a risk. How did I know I would be successful? Had I not taken the chance, I would not have known the joy, satisfaction and benefits of having attended and graduated from college. In addition, it was important to be flexible in changing plans from taking a factory job where I would receive immediate gratification to college attendance where I was prepared for a lifetime career.

Third, I have found that it is essential to include spiritual elements in your plans. When it seemed that there was no way out of a financial crisis, a power beyond me came forth and opened doors that seemed closed. The promise "The Lord will make a way somehow" became a reality. It is reassuring that God is still performing miracles, even in modern times.

Fourth, a person should learn not only how to make a living from his college experience; he/she must also learn how to live. My self-esteem grew by leaps in bounds. During my experience as a barber, I began to develop social and communication skills by interacting or communicating with students who were my customers and who came from all regions of the United States and from various international countries. Sometimes I wonder if those days of listening to the problems of students as I cut their hair might have, in some ways, led to my becoming the counselor educator and researcher that I am today.

One of the most important landmarks in my life was having completed college. This achievement was especially meaningful because attending and completing college was beyond my wildest dreams. I feel fortunate and even lucky that someone, a teacher, identified me as someone who had the intelligence and initiative to succeed in college and in life. While in college, I not only was prepared to make a living, but I learned how to live. In particular, I gained confidence in myself, learned the value of respecting and appreciating others, and learned the value of being a responsible and self-sufficient person.

Throughout my adult life, I have observed hundreds of young people who are lost or confused about their future career directions. Some of them have been a mirror of me before someone stepped up and offered some support and guidance. Many times, I have used my experience in creative ways to help others, as I was helped when I needed it most. This is one way I have been able to repay my teacher, my mentor and my model for improving the quality of my life, even if he had to trick me into attending college.

Lambs, Coyotes, and Counseling Psychologists:
Dialogues on Multiculturalism in the Badlands of Privilege and
Oppression
Susan L. Morrow & Jesse R. Aros

One's personal narrative of oppression evolves in a social context. Therefore, it is appropriate, perhaps even essential, that these narratives are shared in dialogue, providing both authors and readers the opportunity to participate in a mutual meaning-making process about race/ ethnicity and racism, sexism, and heterosexism and homophobia, as well as how those experiences have shaped who we are as counselors, teachers, supervisors, and mentors. The narrative that follows evolved somewhat serendipitously as a result of a letter of recommendation written on behalf of a student. As the two authors, formerly strangers, became colleagues and friends, we embarked upon a process of sharing who we were over the Internet. This narrative is necessarily multivoiced - a quest for understanding each other and ourselves. It represents the personal and professional development of understanding about racism that emerged as we moved beyond the traditional boundaries of colleagueship into sharing deeper feelings and meanings, taking risks, and reconstructing our own identities in the process.

We invite you to travel with us on our shared journey into the future. But first, we offer a glimpse of who we are from our own perspectives.

Jesse: I am a Chicano counseling psychologist and educator and a one-handed version of rather short, squat, everyday *Mestizo* people. I am 37 years old, with four children ages 6, 3, 20 months, and "one on the way." I am one of very few psychologists in the Western Pacific/ Micronesian region. Guam, a past Spanish possession and a current U. S. colony of 140,000, is currently attempting to decolonize, but still in need of psychological liberation, individually and collectively. Which is why I came when asked and have stayed to date.

Sue: I am a 57-year-old White lesbian feminist of German, English, French, and Irish descent, born in Louisiana, raised in California, and matured in Arizona. I am in a 25-year relationship and have two adult children. I am a counseling psychologist, having been a masters-level counselor for 18 years before returning to school for my Ph.D. and defending my dissertation on her 50th birthday. I teach in the counseling psychology program at the University of Utah.

This dialogue begins with our earliest experiences of race/ethnicity and racism, gender and sexism, and heterosexism and homophobia. We discover that we are each lamb and coyote, privileged oppressor and target (we hope not victim) of oppression. We then explore our evolution as activists and how our activism affected our evolution as professionals. Finally, we take a journey into two possible futures, reflecting each of our personal styles, Jesse as pessimist, Sue as optimist, and what we believe are the dilemmas that we must grapple with as multiculturally committed professionals.

What Are Our Earliest Memories of Race, Ethnicity, and Racism?

Jesse: I was about three or four years old and blurted out to my older sister that her Godfather (our great uncle) was "just a dirty old Mexican," and that I was glad "my Godparents were White." I remember denying as a child that I had said that as I got into my own Mexican-ness, propelled from guilt and recognition of my own self-hate.

I remember being four years old and angering my dark brown (*Chilango* brown) cousins by calling them "jungle bunnies" and "spear chuckers." They threw rocks at me while my fairer-skinned cousins tried unsuccessfully to stop them. My Uncle Billy, a blue-eyed and thus rather exotic Mexican *mestizo* came to my aid. The anger and tension has divided the lighter from the darker cousins of my generation until this day.

When did you realize color/ race/ stereotypes? Apparently, I was steeped in it, precocious about it, and strongly influenced by it, "it" meaning racism, color-consciousness, hurtful words, stereotypes, and the like.

Sue: I think you would naturally be precocious about race and color, as it was part of your daily experience and had implications for your identity and safety. I don't think I became aware so early because it wasn't salient to my life when I was young. I was born in Baton Rouge, Louisiana and was raised solely around White folk until high school, when my mom hired a Black maid to do ironing.

I remember cowboys and Indians. When we played in our

neighborhood, I wanted always to be the Indian Princess. I would be exotic, beautiful, and helpless and get stolen away by the cowboys. And the Indian Braves would always get killed. These cowboys were, of course, White cowboys. In those days I did not know Indians could be cowboys too. Race was intertwined in both our lives in very different ways from childhood. For Jesse, race, ethnicity, and color were highly salient very early, while Sue's immersion in White culture and privilege contributed to the invisibility of race and color until much later in her youth. Likewise, our conscious experiences with gender and sexism differed radically.

What Are Our Earliest Memories of Gender and Sexism?

Sue: As I remember the cowboy and Indian play, I am also aware of how entwined my awareness was of myself as a girl. Of course, I didn't understand it then, but look at how I perceived my role--exotic, beautiful, and helpless. What a setup for a future of disempowerment. How do you remember yourself as male when you were really young?

Jesse: (laughs, stops) What I remember about being male when I was three or so is twofold: Getting my butt kicked from another 3 or 4-year-old kid down the street and my mother crying when she saw me, my Dad yelling at me that I'd better learn to fight better than that or that I'd have a whole life of ass-whoopings to look forward to and being fascinated with women' and girls' hair, breasts, and our neighborhood chums' euphemism for heterosexual coitus: "snake in the grass." In fact, the last time I slept in my parents' bed was when I laughingly told my Mom that I had seen Dad's snake in her grass. I don't think I'd turned four yet. Hadn't thought about any of that in years! That's what I remember early on about being male, but how do I remember myself as male when I was really young? Torn. Anxious. Turned on. All at the same time and not really knowing how to handle it all, but knowing instinctively that I had better figure something out real quick in the areas of fighting and sex. Pretty textbook, huh Sue?

Sue: Yeah, textbook. I think the sad thing for me is knowing I was not at all confused about my desire to be cute, helpless, taken care of. That lasted for years and years. Probably still have some of it going on. When I divorced, I remember being terrified because now I would have to take care of myself. I didn't know how, but I learned. And what a robbery it was, too. Now that I am the full-time breadwinner in my relationship, I see what a sense of adequacy was denied me before. What was your first real awareness of sexism?

Jesse: I think I really figured it out watching my mom and dad fight. Mom would not fight Dad or really say anything to him, unless she got real drunk. Then, she'd fight, but pay dearly. It was like a Darwinian thing in my simple 5-year-old head, "might was right," and the neighborhood, the TV, all seemed to confirm it all. How does that nursery rhyme go: "Daddy has money and Mommy has none." Maybe that's another piece of it, or the same piece, but another end? Still, it goes way back.

Sue: Indeed, it goes way back. When I was in 7th grade, I wanted to be a physician. A guy told me that I couldn't be a doctor, because girls were afraid of frogs, and you had to cut up frogs to learn to be a doctor. I decided then not to be a doctor after all. How do you think those early experiences have affected us as adults? In terms of privilege? Power? Oppression?

Jesse: Well, you're a doctor now, no? You're cutting this frog pretty good (smiles). Our early experiences seem to suggest we both bought into and rejected the privilege, the power, the oppression, and still are trying to set things right. Why else would be doing what we're doing?

Sue: Yeah, but what about you? We're both lambs and coyotes, *si?* Did you really reject the privilege of being male? You still have it, you know.

Jesse: *Claro*, both, but not sure privilege is something one can reject. It's more like one needs to not let it go to ones head and must extend the privilege, pass it on. Know what I mean? Though, honestly, it is so much easier for me to focus on what I don't have (*el cordero/* the lamb) than the canines of my privilege, *entiende?*

What Are Our Earliest Memories of Heterosexuality and Homosexuality, of Heterosexism and Homophobia?

Sue: I grew up thinking of myself as heterosexual, so I didn't have to deal with many of the issues that my gay and lesbian brothers and sisters dealt with as children. I think I "did" heterosexuality so well that I felt really good about myself when I came out as a lesbian in my 30s. I know that before college I knew about homosexuals (men), but I can't remember what I knew. We couldn't wear green on Thursdays in elementary school because then we would be "queer," but I don't think I had a sense of what that meant. Only that it was something to be avoided. During my sophomore year at San Jose State, one of the girls in my dorm pointed to two other girls (we called ourselves girls then) and said, "Did you know they are lesbians?" I responded, "What is a lesbian?" My friend responded, "They're like homosexuals, only they're girls." I remember knowing what she meant and being very intrigued. It was only later, in my junior or senior year that I began to understand that my roommates had a real aversion to hugging or touching other girls because they might be mistaken for lesbians. I remember not understanding what the big deal was.

Jesse: Hmmm . . . Heterosexuality, I think I always knew what that was about, in my home, on my street. I remember being 5 or 6 and planning and looking forward in great detail with my best friend Doug (the guy I told you about who kicked my butt when we were 3 or 4) to the time when we could leave home at 16, quit school, get a job for party money and to rent a cheap apartment and have sex with all the "girls" (that's what we called you too back then) and maybe even some "women." Now, homosexuality - that was a different story. I really did not know what that was until I was 7 or 8 and my father hissed about "fags." I didn't know what those were, so I asked. My father told me that they were men who fucked each other. I was incredulous. I was completely not informed, exposed, nor even aware of this dimension, but now knew what my father and other Mexican males meant by terms like *joto* (fag), and *puto* (punk - as in "to be punked"). These I knew were put-downs of fighting and enemy-making proportions, but now I know more about how they were construed and what they meant. That was my first exposure to male homosexuality, from a notably hostile context.

My mother was the only one who talked about lesbians. She used to tell us about how they hit on her in the bus or beach or whatever. As a kid about the same age, I remember thinking that lesbians just had a thing for mothers, but somehow at first thought they were another category of men until my mother re-explained it to me. For me, it was another mind blower from yet another non-supportive source.

Sue: So what changed this for you? You must have had some pretty
         raunchy attitudes towards gays and lesbians as a result of this.
Jesse: Definitely! Between that and my religious background, I
         thought of GLB folks as perverts and used to really get
         verbally abusive when other guys would check me out in
         public restrooms, locker rooms, and etcetera. What changed
         for me? I got an education and started talking with GLB folks
         and found that all those whom I encountered and spoke with at
         New York University were caring, good people that I liked. I
         even found a lot to model in the monogamous relationships of
         several lesbian friends and colleagues like Kris & Sara. I
         guess, simply put, the data did not merit my strong bias, so I
         have mellowed. Though to this day, I still cannot say that I'm
         completely okay with homosexuality. I do not hope that my
         sons will be gay, nor my daughter lesbian. I hope and expect
         heterosexuality for them. There still remains a line around my
         immediate family. It does not bother me that my stepbrother is
         gay, but my child . . . that would bother me. So maybe I've
         changed, but not on all levels. What do you think?
Sue: Jesse, it sounds a lot like if I were to say, "Some of my best
         friends are people of color, but I wouldn't want my daughter to
         marry one." When I came out to my brother Chuck, he said
         almost the same thing: "I don't have any trouble with lesbians,
         but I wouldn't want my daughter to marry one (yuk, yuk)!"
         How do we really heal the divisions among us if we won't let
         our children marry one another?
Jesse: Point well taken--and I still catch myself wanting to "yes, but"
         you here. Weird, huh?
Sue: Jesse, say more.
Jesse: (fidgeting) The struggle is that my schema is fundamentally, at
         the deepest levels, still quite heterosexist, I guess, even
         patriarchal. My take on religion and my culture, my class - I
         find it difficult to go to the point that you are inferring. I find I
         not only move away a little on the GLB issue when it comes to
         my children, but even the thought of my children (and their
         children) mescegenating into mainstream America by
         marrying Whites bothers me. I guess that I want my children
         to only go so far (or is it close?), but I am anxious of them
         becoming lost or not forgetting who they are and what that
         means to us, me, and them. I already have such fixed
         expectations for my four children, even the youngest born

only last week, I'm already starting to reflect on who, what, and how his life will be and it does not (in my own mind anyways) go like that in this anticipatory paternal fantasy of mine. As I listen to myself here, I realize that I'm not speaking in an entirely rational way, though I am trying to be honest and tell you that I seem only to go so far myself when it comes to my hopes for my children's sexual identity, but their ethnocultural and religious identities seem to be there too "hedging the path." Does that help you understand?

Sue: It does and it doesn't. I appreciate you taking the risk of being honest, and if I felt reservations about my kids partnering across race/ ethnic lines I think I would tell you, and it would not feel very good. But what if one of your children *is* pre-gay or pre-lesbian and you inadvertently communicate to her or him that you expect that child to marry and give you grandchildren? Do you know what that does to kids? What if Carlos brings home a Chicano boyfriend some day? No miscegenation there. This is such an important issue - what do you do when your religious views contradict your political ones? How do you reconcile the God-says-it's-wrong thing about homosexuality when you have a political stance of tolerance and advocacy for oppressed groups? And how do I respect cultural values about issues such as homosexuality or gender that appear to me to be harmful? It's been an issue I've struggled with and am not finished with. So now we go to a deeper level with each other. This is very good.

What Were Our Earliest Personal Experiences with Racism, Sexism, and Heterosexism/ Homophobia, and How Did We Emerge as Activists?

Jesse: I remember only flashes and pieces of things from the mid-to-late '60s. When I was four a White teenager stole my tricycle and he wouldn't give it back. I ran crying to my older sister (then seven). She tried to get my bike back. She actually threw a punch and a kick. Tommy beat my sister until her face was bloody, but my sister didn't cry until my parents got her inside. There were other White boys like "Stoner" and Bob, who used to play catch with me (literally). They would go out four or six feet, and one of them would throw me to the other until, one day, Bob dropped me, and all the big White boys ran away, as I had a broken arm. What does all this mean about my early perception of Whites? I don't think I understood them or why they would throw me around and play with me and then disappear when I got hurt. Or why Tommy took my tricycle, teased me so long, and then hit my sister so hard and so many times. I don't think I had a schema or philosophy yet, just confusion. What about you, Sue? What was your first recollection of racism?

Sue: I know now that I was steeped in racism - my own and that of White people who were part of my context. I think my first conscious awareness came when my family moved to Alhambra, California when I was in fourth grade. On the way we spent a few days with my parents' friends in El Paso. I remember being very confused because I had said or done something inappropriate (from the point of view of my mom's friend) in relationship to a Mexican maid - gotten too friendly or something, and my mom's friend told me, "We don't do that." I asked my Mom later, and she explained that in Texas it was like in Louisiana, only with Mexicans instead of Negroes. I understood, so I must have known about segregation - oh, yeah, I remember knowing there were separate public restrooms and drinking fountains for Blacks and not understanding why. I remember thinking it was especially strange about Mexicans because they looked like us (my whole family had very dark hair and eyes, and my dad had dark skin - I don't think I distinguished Mexicans from our family by appearance).

Jesse: Picture it, my good colleague, it's August 16, 1979, and I am working at a local butcher shop in LA saving for college. I go to try and unplug an upsurge of meat coming up the neck of a very old and very messed-up grinder. Did a dumb thing, didn't unplug the electric cord; power surges; machine leaps; fingers get caught in auger, feeding them and the hand, wrist, and part of the forearm into the knife blades and against the plate of the grinder. I turn it off, all us Brown folks were scared white, no lie! Paramedics came, one fainted, the other vomited, and then I knew I was in deep *Kim chi*. I go to the hospital, lose 11 pints of blood, get transfusions, stabilize, and get kicked out three days later after getting caught by my nurse in a one-handed push-up contest.
         A few weeks later the critical incident really unfolds. The whole purpose of wrapping the amputated stump is to get it to

take well to prosthesis. So, into Massey's prosthetic shop I go, and this mustached Captain Kangaroo-looking guy shows me the place. I spent almost an hour looking at boxes and closet racks filled with plaster of Paris and metal molds of hands, missing fingers, limb stumps, artificial eyes, and prostheses while this White guy is telling me details of each of these stories. As I write this I can see the boxes and even remember some of the names and stories: Davis - a Black machinist who lost a finger on a drill press in a metal press; Gonzalez, "another" Mexican kid working on a meat grinder who lost much more of his arm than I did; Fernandez, a Mexican kid who was industrially dismembered. I remember thinking when in the fuck am I going to see a White person's stump mold and hear about how they were dismembered? And the last thing I'm shown and told about is this little pathetic mold, a shrunken small nubby stump. I felt bad, sick, and even sympathetic - and Dr. Massey begins to tell me about "little Suzie" who lives in Idaho and was born "this way." And he went on in a hushed and reverent tone about how little Suzie climbs mountains and what a brave little trooper she is.

I leave this little hell with my mind reeling from the names on the boxes and what it meant to me - Fernandez, Gonzalez, Mendez, Garcia, Aros - all these Mexican kids in our teen years who were injured and how we were talked about so matter-of-factly. You know, come to think of it, Mr. Davis, the Black machinist, was spoken about in the same tone as we were, but his piano-playing skills and need for a finger to do that was much harped on about. But, oh, little Suzie - that was it, she seemed to matter the most - a poor innocent White girl who "was born that way." No euphemisms were wasted on any of us else, just direct blow-by-blow accounts.

I left there thinking that something really was fundamentally wrong with the world. Massey's implied messages screamed out at me that I was indeed part of a very great number of folks seen as "dispensable." My accident was and is an almost normative thing for my ethnicity, my class. I can honestly say to you, Sue, that this experience in the prosthetic shop really got me into what I am doing now in the field.

Sue: Your stories of coming to awareness about race and ethnicity and racism are scary and disturbing - another level in our communication. They touch a place in me that says, "Am I worthy of this sharing?" Also of wondering if it's okay to ask you to go to this place of pain. Will healing follow? Do I have a core so deep to share with you? I have my own pain related to other things, but this? I realize here that, no matter what struggles may be mine from a White perspective about race/ethnicity/racism, I cannot go there with you to those deep places except in my care for you, my hope that our relationship can provide the kind of support that will make going to those places okay.

Jesse: What I don't get is the "worthiness" issue. What makes you think you do not deserve to hear what I want to tell you? Not wanting to hear, I understand. I often don't want to think of how others' perceptions about race/ color/ racism still affect me. The pain is there, whether we talk or not or I pay attention to it or not. The out-group experience is like phantom pain. First, trauma happens and you learn that you are now esteemed to be less than what you are because some part is lost, removed, ignored, devalued. And the pain that happens is real yet occurs in places and ways that you cannot get to physically to heal. Like when my stump aches, or worse, my right hand or palm itches, I just cannot scratch it - it doesn't exist in that plane. I have to pay attention to the pain or itch and tell myself that it is happening and that it will happen again; I must allow it to happen, or the itch or pain gets worse. Sometimes ignoring it in short bursts is okay, but in the long term, the itch and pain in my stump will intensify, much like my experiences as a member of an out-group cannot be ignored for too long without affecting who and what I am and how I feel. What is your pain? How did "they" hurt you? Who told you that you were "less than," not right," "handicapped"? How did/do you feel/respond? Perhaps the scariest part of this paper is sharing our pain, shame, and anger that are attached to our "catching on" about our own disenfranchisements and entitlements. This is really hard. Think about it. You are White, I am *Raza*. You are a woman, I am a man. You are gay and I am straight. You are physically "whole," I am not. You are secular, I am religious. We have different disenfranchisements and entitlements, and we are trying to write them--not about them. For the sake of this paper, there is the race, color, and racism thing; but in the real world between us, there are all of these issues swirling between and within.

We have hope and faith that we can connect, but there is no sure knowledge and maybe even mixed findings in our historical records. Face it, Sue, at any number of levels, we've had turns as both the coyote and the lamb, both of whom have now sat down together and decided to tell each other our story and to be friends, co-authors even. What a change, historically speaking, no?

Sue: Yeah. And good point about the worthiness issue. What's that all about? White guilt? It's not about not wanting to hear, even though it's hard and makes me sad. Maybe it's not about worthiness at all, but a sense of awe at being let into your world - I think humility might be a more apt word. Like I've been given a great gift. When a story told to me by someone (like you) resonates strongly with a similar story of mine, it builds a bridge across whatever barriers have been erected by society. This goes to the place of my pain. How "they" hurt me. "They" were other girls in Louisiana who judged me not good enough. I don't know why. There I was, somewhat socially inept, with curly, curly brunette hair that frizzed in the humidity. Later, in the '60s, I had my hair long and permed it straight. In the '70s I reclaimed my curls and grew an Afro-- not a bad one for a White girl. So I digress, as is healthy when dealing with old pain, I suspect. The blonde girls (was there even one dark-hair among them?) whispered behind my back. I've told you about eating my lunch alone on the high school steps. I retreated to the library across the street from my school, devoured everything in sight. I remember a book that had a wonderful story about a girl who was all bruised and hurt, and she found herself in a room with a wonderful magic woman (witch?) who plunged her into a bottomless basin of healing water and made her okay. I can't find it now, but it was wonderful and healing. About the coyote and the lamb: I keep asking myself to go deeper about my coyote part in relation to racism. I think the empathy that evolved because of my own pain helped to insure that I never was purposely racist. But I think much of what I have perpetrated has been so unconscious and yet so hurtful to people of color. All those unconscious, insensitive things still at the level of unawareness - coyote.

Jesse: As I read your story, I am struck that phenotypically you weren't "quite White" to these pale, blond, small people, who were/ are the societal "icons" of White femaleness.

Sue: I also have what kids in school called "slanty" eyes--full eyelids that squint when I smile or laugh. Kids were always asking me if I was Chinese. So in Louisiana I was somehow ethnic to these kids. I've also as an adult been asked if I am Jewish. I have what I'd call a "dark German" look--although my skin is light, my hair and eyes are dark and could be anything.

Jesse: I've often wondered if I'd be E-mailing you from my office if I was as smooth brown as or browner than my Dad. I like to think I would, but I doubt it. Truth is, no *Chilango*-brown *Raza* males from my high school went to college.

Sue: In so many ways my childhood was the opposite of yours - living in a lower-middle-class White neighborhood, playing with my best friend Penny across the street, it all looks idyllic. But then I remember a dawning realization of my own difference as an abused child from my peers, their gradual withdrawal from me because I was, as I look back, a little odd. If I had been my teacher, I surely must have known something was wrong at home, the poor little waif. I've told you about the loneliness that surrounded my high school years in Louisiana. I believe this was partly my own social tenuousness because of the abuse in my household, part class - we did not have old family or old money in the South.

Later I did the college thing (it was assumed I'd go to college, get my bachelors', become a teacher or nurse so I'd have something to fall back on if my husband died). My mom died during my sophomore year; I went home to take care of my family; my dad remarried; I went back to school, became involved in civil rights, met my husband, became a teacher, married, taught in inner city schools, marched on Washington, quit teaching, had two kids (the lights of my life), joined the peace movement, and then . . .

I found feminism. It changed my life. I spoke in public for the first time without painful shyness. I fell in love with a woman. I came out. My husband took my kids. This is what oppression means to me. I was a "super mom" - had my children via natural childbirth, breastfed, made their baby food myself, learned everything there was to learn about child raising, stayed home with them except for taking an occasional university class, and he took them away because I was a lesbian. Some time later I became involved with doing workshops and visiting women in prison, and I watched, when visiting hours were up, as these women's mothers and sisters and husbands took their screaming babies and children away from them, and those women couldn't shed a tear. And I, too, learned that the only way to tolerate that level of pain, to lose your babies, was never to cry, never to give in to the pain, to become numb. The price I paid for that numbness was the recurrent nightmare of taking my kids to the doctor, sending them in ahead of me, and being raped in the parking lot. Jesse, where does all this take us? How do I juggle my own pain/oppression in the context of my commitment not to get into "My pain is worse than your pain," not to silence ethnic voices? I've been oppressed as a woman, as a heavy woman, as a middle-aged woman, as a lesbian. I've been ignored at meetings where men dominate. I've had a boy yell at me from the street, "Hey, fatso," and walked into a classroom to teach only to see a message on the blackboard, "Save a whale; kill a fat chick." I was told, when I wanted to apply to graduate school, that it would be a waste of their time to take someone my age. I've lost my children's childhood. I've had friends and family turn their backs on me when I came out (or outed by my husband) as a lesbian.

Jesse: I have had such a good life, but it has been hard for me sometimes. Still, I realize that I am fortunate/ lucky/ blessed; my trials have been tame by many of my/our cohorts' (or even earlier generations of the Aros clan here in the U. S. and Mexico) experiences and standards. Now, about *you*, hmm . . .? You . . . look inward and outward and find what's there. My guess is that you'd be surprised at what you may find in each slice of your identity and being as well as the "gestalt" or interactions of the "slices." Remember, we can be both lambs *and* coyotes. Think of my male privileges, how I earn more for the same or even less work, quantitatively, qualitatively, focus the ills on/ around me in your responses. Think of times you have been intimidated, shamed, hurt because of all the bullshit that has been artificially and socially constructed vis-à-vis an XX versus XY chromosomal presence. Dig deep . . .

Sue, I think that you are really onto something: It is not about my pain versus yours. (Isn't that where we have gotten sidetracked as a profession?) It is about our pain: We change sides as oppressors and oppressed and *that* is what makes it all so uncomfortable. Think about it: Being who you are cost you the removal of your own children from your side. Why do I think that was not an isolated incident? When was the last time we talked about the scope of this pain in our multicultural meetings? Our anger is appropriate, understandable, and isn't it the pain that is the catalyst and the non-reducible entity that links our anger, shame, fear, guilt? All of us as people, notwithstanding our own professionalism, are skilled at "burying" the weightier issues. Our failure, individually and collectively, to go deep and turn our "counselor beams" upon ourselves as oppressed and oppressors, privileged and disenfranchised, may well prove to be the undoing of authentic and real multiculturalism, let alone progress towards our own cross-cultural, or even transcultural, understanding.

Sue: Some of what I think has always gone wrong about the intersection of racism and the other "isms" is that we have approached it all from a liberal standpoint, where everyone wants a piece of the pie. Now, the pie can be economic goods, or whatever, but my experience is that the real pie for real people is attention to their pain. So when people of color give voice to their pain, everyone else tries to get on the bandwagon--"but what about my pain?" - and when women try to address their pain over sexism, men start talking about how hard it is to be a man. Fact is, we each benefit from the oppression of others, yet what we've been doing in response is to inadequately deal with each group's pain and oppression without *really* hearing them, without *really* addressing the issues, and without *really* changing. In our efforts to hear everybody, nobody has been heard more than superficially. But the flip side, when we hear someone else's pain about their oppression, it triggers our own, and our own needs to be heard as well. As I remember the original Multicultural Conference and Summit and the panel they had about "Difficult Dialogues," I am struck by how lesbian/ gay issues were - or were not - dealt with. The panel included Michael Brown, an African American fundamentalist Christian, and Laura Brown, a Jewish lesbian, among others. A core issue was that Michael said he didn't really call himself a multiculturalist because he could not support lesbian/gay people because of his religion. And Laura said she wasn't asking for advocacy, but just asked that he not overtly oppress her/us. I am reminded of Sarah Grimke, a feminist and Quaker who wrote in 1838: "I ask no favors for my sex. I surrender not our claim to equality. All I ask of our brethren is that they take their feet off our necks, and permit us to stand upright on the ground which God has designed us to occupy." On one level, I agreed with Laura; but I also believe we all must come to grips with our prejudice, regardless how we justify it. I think it is unconscionable to use the same scripture that once was used to condone slavery to deny equal rights to lesbians and gays. I have really struggled with this over the years, and it's interesting that I always feel I need to silence my own voice as a White lesbian when I am in multicultural circles, because many people of color have seen LGB issues as a White thing. But then, an African American lesbian woman stood up during the question/ comment period at the end of that session and spoke of her invisibility as a lesbian at this conference. There had been just one part of one session dedicated to LGB issues, and now a brother African American was justifying not being able to support the full humanness and equality of this woman. I've been thinking a lot about the coyote-lamb metaphor. I find it so much easier to think and talk about my experiences of learning to become a multicultural person--or even to explore my past pain - than to examine my own racism. I feel my greatest transgressions around racism and classism were related to being an inner-city schoolteacher. I think your stories make me aware of how vulnerable children are and how I may have harmed my students through my own ignorance. I feel a lot of shame about that. However, as I often tell my students, "White guilt is a waste of time." I believe that if I am doing something to create change, I don't need to hang out in shame or guilt (the flip side of "If you're not part of the solution, you're part of the problem"). This leads to my experiences, the critical incidents in my life that served as catalysts to my becoming an activist. There were a series of important events starting with joining a civil rights club in college, then choosing to teach in inner-city schools in St. Louis and Detroit in my first career as an elementary-school teacher. The real life-changing event occurred one year when the father of one of my students invited me and my husband to go with him to the second Poor People's March on Washington in the '60s. We drove out from Detroit, slept in his car under the watchful eye of the National Guard, and marched - all colors of people. A young Black man took my hand at one point and said, "Thanks, sister!" Jesse Jackson led the march, and Coretta Scott King spoke (this was after Dr. King's assassination). I was forever changed. We went back home and participated in Black-White consciousness-raising groups. It was also the beginning for me of integrating race/ethnicity into my teaching, although at a very primitive level. I was teaching in a Lutheran elementary school and began asking the children to draw pictures of a Jesus who looked like them.

How Did Our Experiences of Race/Ethnicity and Racism Shape Who We Are as Professionals?

Jesse: How does all this shape me as a counselor? It actually caused me to want to stop the pain, anger, hate, shame of being afflicted and to set the oppressors right. Got a story. Wanna hear it?

Sue: Sure!

Jesse: I sat in a psycholinguistics course as a junior in college and was introduced to the race, "g" factor, and fairness-in-testing debate via an interesting and related tangent to a lecture. I called my dad later that night and told him about what I had heard. He told me that he had heard that as a kid in junior high science class and that he was disappointed, but not surprised. Ergo, I concluded that there was a whole lot of misunderstanding about how/ what/ why/ who we non-Whites are that needed to be cleared up and that my community needed me to join this fray. I wanted to, and badly, because of my shock, anger, and disbelief at how even good science is so readily perjured by interpretations and preconceptions. That's why I'm into research methods, psychometrics, and trait-factor psychology.

Sue: I had always found psychometrics and assessment boring until I met Elsie Moore, an African American professor at ASU, who began to help me understand their importance. Stuff like that becomes important when it relates to real people and justice. You've asked me what it is that makes me interested in diversity, what makes me care. My answer is really a question: "What is it about a White counselor, supervisor, or faculty member that makes it possible for her/ him to become a culturally competent individual?" My education in multicultural counseling - as well as ongoing continuing education in community building, conflict resolution, and multicultural issues - certainly have contributed tremendously to my evolution. However, there's no substitute for experience, in the form of both my earlier activism and now my experiences working with colleagues, clients, and students around multicultural issues. My own development in that area became really clear to me when I counseled a Mexican American woman client raised in a mining town in the Southwest. As we explored the source of her depression, it became clear to me that racism was an important contributor to her depression. When I first asked her directly about this, she denied any experiences of racism in her life. I backed off until about a month later, when she raised the issue. In fact, she had experienced depression off and on since junior high school, when she and another Mexican American girl were shunned by their elementary school White girlfriends. It was healing and empowering for her to identify how powerful that unnamed racism had been in her life. I also feel I am coming of age as I work as a supervisor with our practicum students. I integrate a multicultural perspective by helping students identify their own and their clients' stages of ethnic or White identity development and examine how those stages affect therapy. As a teacher and researcher, my work has become increasingly multiculturally focused, particularly over the last four years. I've moved from "just add color and stir" to a place of greater and greater infusion of issues related to diversities of all kinds as well as addressing issues of power and privilege. What about you?

Jesse: I came to a Brown university to teach all I can to combat the "g" factor, race, and IQ shit and to bring folks into the system who will promote and understand the salience and valence of individual differences by environment over genetic factors. I know I am here to train competent counselors who can recognize when developmental factors have been breached or ignored, such as folks who want to create vocational and academic tracks for students in junior high or earlier based on GPA and DAT + CPQ scores without analyzing career development and without measuring career maturity and related factors. This in turn seriouslycircumscribes subsequent interest and ability development by narrowing types of input and stimulation before adequate exploration can take place. As a result, we have lots of Brown folks being pushed into vocational education, training them to be gardeners, cashiers, or bookkeepers. What a waste!

Sue: We both want so much to make a difference, to have our institutions and our profession become more responsive. Wonder what turns our field will take over the next decade or so?

It is now the year 2013. Sue and Jesse "met" by telephone in 1995 and continued an E-mail friendship until 2005, when Jesse finally moved from Guam to the mainland to accept a faculty position in the West. Since then, they have met regularly at professional conferences. This meeting is the 13th National Multicultural Conference and Summit, originally hosted by the presidents of Divisions 17 (Counseling), 35 (Women), and 45 (Ethnic Minority) of APA in 1999. That was also the year that the president of APA, Dick Suinn, and the presidents of all three divisions were people of color, and the conference commemorated that achievement as well as bringing multiculturalists together. The following August, the opening ceremony of APA was a cultural mosaic with Jesse Jackson as keynote speaker. The Multicultural Conference and Summit has become a regular event and one that continues to address the complexities of multicultural work.

Sue turned 70 this year and is still going strong. She keeps threatening to retire from her faculty position, where she is program director for the third time, but her love for her work and students keep her going. "One more year," she promises. She arrives at the opening social with a flourish, wearing a purple velvet pantsuit, dangling amethyst earrings, and her trademark Doc Martens boots. Having fought a few academic battles elsewhere, won by the skin of his proverbial teeth, Jesse has founded a program in *Aztlan* that is big, bold, and tough enough to handle his passion, dry humor, and unruly spirit. Still blessed with his thrift-store wardrobe of string ties, old dress shirts, and khaki baggies; heavily-muscled peasant physique; central-city twang; and ethnic good looks, Jesse is occasionally mistaken by new graduate students for the college's janitor rather than one of its associate deans, a fact he continues to be paradoxically both concerned about and a little pleased.

Two scenarios follow, reflecting the personality styles of each of us. Jesse is the pessimist, or, as he might put it, realist. He does not expect much from the multicultural future, as he has observed the academic backbiting and selling out for so many years that he sometimes despairs of ever seeing real change. As the curtain rises, Jesse's future scenario plays out.

Jesse: With the mild sun of Redondo Beach barely warming my balding and now shaved-smooth pate, I catch my reflection going into the Conference. "You look just like a one-handed Chicano Clement Vontress," I say to myself. Chuckling at the thought of having compared myself to one of the original *gerentes* (bosses) in the field, I remember him saying that we could become ghettoized as we create professional bodies for ourselves as psychologists and counselors of color. I feel my brow knit and my face go smooth like a door. "Look where you are, *Viejito*," I hear myself say, *"al mero barrio profesional, que lindo*--in the middle of the professional ghetto, how beautiful it is!" as I survey the plush surroundings of this still rich, White part of the comparatively still rich, White Western part of my hometown: *Nuestra Señora de la Reina de los Angeles de Alta California.*

I feel my eyes tearing up a little. I remember how tough it was when I worried about leaving my barrio, leaving my family's selected college major for me; I wondered if I would become a *vendido.* I fought it, the push to assimilate. I got my training and both kept and challenged aspects of myself, my culture, my gender, my religion, everything. In the end, I was still *Raza*, male, religious, still me, but "different." Even afterwards, as a brand-new professor I cried for a few weeks at night all alone, as my family slept on, until I came to the conclusion that I had not sold out but had sold my place of comfort for what I hope is the eventual good of my community. Walking in autopilot, my mind goes back to the time when my father and I were escorted from Rancho Palos Verdes all the way to Wilmington. My Dad took me there in 1970 to motivate me by showing me how folks lived outside of the barrio. "Rancho Palos Verdes is only a few miles south of here," I think, "Funny how we come here to celebrate our diversity in the same kind of beach community that so often rejects us--what's that about?" I trip over a pile rug and stumble, but do not fall. "So much for auto-pilot," I mutter to myself in English, "I'll have to answer that question later." Deciding to leave my autistic world and focus on what is going on around me for reasons of physical safety and perhaps to reduce my own anxiety of being both within and without "my turf," I am heading toward the ballroom where the opening social is to be held. Sue and I have agreed to meet, have a drink of something, socialize, and escape to Los Angeles with some of our students to have real food. The efforts of the hotel to provide a multicultural cuisine are admirable, but within train shot of the "real thing," we can't bear to compromise. I sense someone watching me and look up. It's Sue! She was listening to me mutter, I can tell by the smile on her face. Busted, I laugh; and after we exchange our usual few dozen *abrazos* and quips, we escape, students in tow. We talk as we head for the train.

Sue: You know, Jesse, when I went to the first of these conferences, it was such a thrill. You know, everyone (almost) on the same side of things, a feeling of shared purpose, a belief that everything we were struggling for would come to be. I think I even saw some progress in those days, yet look, today at the conference I heard the same old things. The marginalization of people who don't toe the party line. A sense of discouragement and bitterness on the part of people who had so much energy 15 years ago! (Jesse, I don't believe this is going to happen, but I'm trying to get into it.) It feels like we have had so much talent, energy, and hope go down the drain, and although there are a few "model" training programs here and there, for the most part it's status quo.

Jesse: (Talking to Sue, while the students listen intently to the almost legendary curmudgeon) Yes, the thrill was there then and yet there was a quiet undertow I don't think anyone talked about publicly. You remember, we were all moved by the beautiful and powerful words, but it was so *hard* to implement and change things at the systemic level, especially when everyone (at least the White folks, almost all of them) was now a "convert" singing praises to Derald Wing Sue and Thomas Parham and all the major players back then and there were *plenty*! Specialists and converts--in frickin' droves--all climbing up on the multicultural bandwagon! Remember that, Sue? Maybe we *did* multiculturalism before we *were* multicultural, do you know what I'm saying? That's what I think Fred Leong and Helen Kim were trying to say when they wrote about getting beyond the sensitization piece, but we were all caught up in the hype and couldn't hear them. (Jesse shakes his shaved head and looks down at the monorail floor as it speeds towards Central City, away from the Westside, and then he looks up) About now, I think you are right, the movers and shakers are tired. I am tired. It is so hard to effect change in a system when everybody (individually or programmatically) thinks that they are at the level of "integration" in their ethnic identity development. When in fact, there's now Chaos theory-based statistical data that strongly suggest that the archaic fundamental attribution error seems to affect the simultaneous cause-effect attribution processes we make in evaluating and endorsing our own identity developmental processes, bias   reduction algorithms notwithstanding. The fundamental attribution error has a corollary here and   continues to raise its ugly head and we are finding that most individuals overestimate their own ethnic identity development and underestimate others' for the same exact reasons. So what do you think? (The students blink at one another with some confusion. The monorail has just passed Crenshaw Blvd.).

Sue: I guess what that raises for me is the whole question of what it is we've been focusing on all this time. Certainly a celebration of diversity, an appreciation for the mosaic of experience we call multiculturalism. And an obsession with identity models, and you're right, we always think we're doing better than we are, and that is scary to me, for example, that you might not tell me when you see through the facade I have built to make myself believe I am not so racist. (Students get very serious and a little nervous.) But I think the point is that White folks have always had so much trouble "going there"--to racism, that is. We'll do celebrations of diversity and learn the basics of counseling people of color, but we won't do oppression. I guess that's one of the reasons we have landed where we are today. I wonder what would have happened if all of us would have embraced the difficult struggle of racism 15 years ago…

Jesse: (Looking at the students, now deathly silent) "Utopia, but there is no such place, *a menos todavia que no*. ("What does that last part mean?" the other students whisper in stereo to the

Chicano student in their midst. The student squirms and answers, "I'm not sure" and looks down--the monorail passes over Hoover by 18th Street. Looking sadly yet tenderly at the Chicano student, Jesse speaks) It means "at least not yet," but that is not quite it either, the essence of ethereality is hard to convey in the translation. (Jesse's mind goes back to Barrio 18 that we were now in; he used to live there for a while when he came back from NYU with his MA in Counseling, as there was no room at Estrada Courts in East Los Angeles. He remembers waking up with rats on his chest, sleeping on the floor, looking for a counseling job that would allow him to counsel folks and not just "manage" them. Sue is watching, brow knit, concerned, wondering . . .) I am sorry, Sue I was tripping, I used to live around here (pointing below) before I went to the Midwest to finish up and get the APA accredited Ph.D. Back to racism. If White folks had a tough time "going there," I think many of us had a tougher time expressing what it was really like to be there at the level of what it did internally to us, know what I mean? (Sue is silent, she knows there's a little more that needs to come out and is waiting). Sue, it's like you saw at those conferences you were telling us about, but the tougher parts were not just the external racism, but how tiny bits of the *mugre/* filth of it becomes internalized in the tiny nooks and crannies deep within the "guts" of one's soul, notwithstanding all of the "airing" and psychic house-cleaning that we do for ourselves as part of self-care and well-being. (Sue nods knowingly, a glint of tear forming in her left eye; seeing it Jesse feels the glint of one or two in his own, but the students stare ahead and we cannot tell what they understand or feel--embarrassment? Or can they share our sadness? Jesse looks at the students.) When I was a pre-doc intern, written on the far corner of a Men's room wall very lightly in pencil was this: "Mexicans are living proof that Indians did f--- buffalo." (Students gasp) This is an example of good old-fashioned overt individual, and perhaps institutional, external, non-internalized racism. All this does is justifiably anger and motivate one to fight for civil rights and human dignity, but . . . (*con tremolo*) the internalized tiny bits of racism that have really gotten in our way are much more insidious. *Fíjate* (looking at Sue), remember when I told you what my Dad said to me as I left for college? (Sue nods; the students look on.) He said, "You are just another dumb-fucking Mexican who should not leave the slaughterhouse." My father, who had always pushed for me to go to school, vomited that horrendous internalized message - from his father? Or God knows where - that festered somewhere in his heart or his wounded soul. When I heard it, I knew what it was and yet it hurt me, too - much more than anybody or anything else could because it came from within, from a very human hero in my past and present. I have dealt with this in counseling, consultation, meditation, prayer, ceremony, and fasting, and yet there are probably still microns of this floating around that I believe may initiate self-doubts in myself as my being a modestly accomplished and competent psychologist and an academic, even now. (Looking at the students) Do you all hear what I am saying here? We all had and have so much painful racism as oppressed, oppressors, and both within us that to embrace the fact that we are lambs and coyotes *ambos/* both. This is where we would not, not could not, "go"--into our multiple identities. (Looking back at Sue) Just like we wrote about around the turn of the century. (I smile, remembering.) Remember, Sue?"

Sue: I remember. (We both smile through our tears) Again, your pain reminds me of my own. You see why I need to believe in a more positive future.

Jesse: *Todos quisimos decir que fuimos puro corderos sin embargo en parte fuimos coyote o lobo tambien/* All of us wanted to say that we were pure lambs, but in part we were coyote or wolf also, just like we wrote about. Glad to know we made such a big impact, huh? Not! (With Sue and Doc Aros intently engaged, both still notice that the students are animatedly engaged in discussing the new Taco Bell Hawai'ian mango chutney bean burrito with oregano sprouts accented with fat-free melted garlic and rosemary butter. Distracted, Jesse tries to refocus as his colon writhes in agony at the unceremonious and forced union of individually and historically awesome ingredients and sauces supplanted from Pacific, Mexican, and Mediterranean cuisines. Shuddering, they continue . . . Remember when we wrote about lambs, coyotes, and counseling psychologists back at the turn of the century, *hermana*? We tried to remind them about the distinct possibility that we might not have dealt with our "isms" above all our own mental colonialism, just like so many of the early folks around us tried to warn us about, *que no?* (Sue nods as the nouvelle fast food banter drones on). We didn't ever think that it could happen to us, the multicultural specialists we were? (Jesse looks down at the floor of the train.) Through our not being able to cooperate, respectfully hear, and fully address each other because of our own unresolved shit plus all that competitive, competitive, competitive, self-aggrandizing, *presumido* "Me Generation" American/Western academic bullshit, I think too many of us acted just like "The Man" we all or too many of us used to commiserate about, for damn good reason, but now, . . . how ironic, *que no?* (Jesse's voice crackles with sadness and anger that amplify his hoarse whisper. The students are silent now, with Doc Aros still looking down, muttering to himself yet audible to those in the rows around him.) We tried to go around the last bits instead of trying to deal with them *y nuestros pinches pendejismos ya nos fagaron/* and our fucking damn idiocies beat us - as it were - with sticks.

As the train pulls to a stop in Union station, some students rush eagerly through the door, while others, more cautious, hang back, waiting for their elders to guide them. Is that very caution something we have instilled in our efforts to guide them as students and as multiculturally competent counselors and counseling psychologists? Is this caution stepping off into unfamiliar territory a sign of their lingering desire for political correctness? Is this all we have accomplished over the past 13 years, that they are still afraid? Sue disembarks, followed by Jesse and the remaining students, and looks back at them, shaking her head.

Sue: We've been here before, countless journeys in which we reinvent the wheel of political correctness, hold back for fear of showing our ignorance, become mired in guilt over what we have not done. Enough!" (Curtain falls, leaving Jesse and the students bewildered.)

As the curtain rises again, Sue and Jesse are seated at a table in one of their favorite haunts on Olvera Street. The students, having tired of listening to the old folks reminisce; have ventured out on their own, all having agreed to meet back at Union Station at the agreed-upon time.

Sue: You know, Jesse, I was just thinking about where the whole multicultural movement could have gone. It could have become polarized so easily, with nobody really hearing anyone else, with different groups cowering off in their own corners, licking their battle wounds and crying out their anger. It could have continued with each group having its own private agenda, the whole "my oppression is worse than your oppression," with everyone vying for a piece of the same pie, not recognizing that the pie of limited   quantities was at its core a rotten pie. But, at some point, something changed. I think the turning point in all of this stuff about multiple oppressions was when, in about 2000, we began to really hear people. We began to talk about what it meant to be lambs *and* coyotes at once, to lay, as my friend Freda Ginsberg suggested, both our privileges and our oppressions on the table. Somewhere in the early years of the 21st century, we began to be more deliberate about listening, supporting, and acting. It took a lot of us analyzing what was going wrong, teaching, learning, and recommitting ourselves to the complicated changes that have to happen. And underneath it all, Jesse, I think it was a commitment we each had to make to our own healing from our own private pain that allowed us to be witnesses to the pain of others, especially those we oppress, without descending into the hell of guilt and shame.

Jesse: (Smiling from the eloquent analysis) Yep, that's what made the difference. Everybody finally realized that the lingering stench of all that oppressive shit wasn't necessarily just coming from one's neighbor; we had all tracked some in, if not produced a little ourselves. (Sue laughs; Jesse continues, more serious now) That was a tough time when we all thought we were experts just because we had hopped up on the multicultural bandwagon. Luckily, we woke up before we really sold out.

Sue: It's interesting to me that my analysis of what happened is all about how we stopped fighting for pieces of the pie, and yours is about how people stopped selling out. Each of us from our own personal framework is unraveling the knots that kept us tied up for so many years. What do you think got people to stop selling out? How do these two pieces - and others - relate?

Jesse: (Tossing his head back and laughing) Sue, you don't miss much, do you? Let me try and explain myself a little more clearly here. To me, cutthroat competitiveness among a group with a collectivistic agenda is prima facie evidence of selling out. To make it worse, the longer one stays in that kind of knot, the more of our multicultural agenda and our individual and collective selves become lost. And I didn't even touch the collectivistic parts of many of us, culturally speaking . . . (Scratching his head now, Jesse looks up at Sue and scowls.) Didn't answer all of what you are asking here, *que no*?

Sue: (Shaking her head) Huh-uh.

Jesse: I think what kept us from selling out is that at the turn of the century we just got so damn tired of the implicit B.S. that when some us finally said "That's enough!" the rest of us really resonated to the cry for personal and professional healing and reform. Those who didn't, well, let's say that they picked up another research interest (laughing delightedly).

Sue: That doesn't do it for me, Jesse. What realization, what awareness or what "clicked" and got people thinking differently?

Jesse: (More serious) What did it for everybody? I don't know. Even regarding myself, I don't think it was the thinking that changed, as much as the willingness to take stock and say "Hey, I'm not liking what I see or hear about these pieces of myself, my part, and that I'm going to change my being and my doing, irregardless of the implications this may have on my career, my popularity, image, etc." Then, it went interpersonal from intrapsychic, spiritual, whatever, then, a "critical mass" effect, perhaps we imploded and it was good? That's my best guess. What do you think, Sue?

Sue: For me, it was recycling the same old processes over and over and watching people leave the Movement (feminist, multicultural, gay, whatever) in pain and anger. Watching old peaceniks become yuppies, lesbian and gay activists become luppies and guppies (Jesse laughs). . . And quite suddenly it became clear there had to be another answer besides replaying this same CD over and over and over. For me, change is a process of a honeymoon phase; then the beginnings of either distress or boredom that accelerate, along with efforts to resolve the problem that also accelerate; then a period of relative hopelessness in which I give up. There's probably a more spiritual definition for this process. But in the giving up, letting go, there is space for a spark of creativity. I think we had reached that frustration point so many, many times without letting go, because we were too desperate for the change. I know I often went home from meetings angry, frustrated, and unhappy, hopeless that we would ever get past the divisiveness, the silencing. In that hopelessness and inertia I remembered what I tell my supervisees about effective therapy: "If at first you don't succeed, change your strategy." It was time to search for a new way of thinking and relating around multiculturalism. I believe a whole lot of us hit that wall around the same time. I remember you did, too. It was like a collective consciousness shift, as you said. The Hundredth Monkey . . .

Jesse: The hundredth monkey - yeah, *me cae bien*. Looking back is so much easier. Hmm . . . growing pains, most of us took it to the next phase. Reminds me of an old Isley Brothers' song "Take me to the next phase . . .Take my soul to the next phase . . .." (Sue nods her assent, old Jess continues). For us, I guess what's "happening" is the next phase. Sure as hell would hate to go back, huh? The only thing is, how are we ever going to fully describe that primeval bullshit to our trainees and younger colleagues? I mean, I had to look at my own privilege as a straight man as well as my oppressed Chicano and disabled parts. You had to face your Whiteness, remember in the late 90s when we met, you wouldn't even capitalize "White" as a proper noun and you were not alone! Hardly anyone did then, remember? Plus, you sure as hell had tons of shit to deal with being out and an advocate for tolerance in Salt Lake City and a long way before that. You, me, most of us, we finally got it, didn't we? The hundredth monkey, the sound of one hand clapping, the opening of our minds, it really happened, didn't it? (Sue nods, smiling, sensing that the religious piece of her old predictable friend is about due for an airing.) Thank the Gods! (Sue casts a glance, old Doc Aros chuckles) Thank the Goddesses too. Just one last thing, and I promise to shut up so we can eat. Even if we find a way to do justice to describing how strained, awkward, and frustrating it used to be in the multicultural camp and why we changed, who will believe us who wasn't there when it happened?
          (Drop Curtain, raise on the present)

Sue: Yeah, and who will believe any of this? That a straight Christian disabled Chicano and a lesbian pagan able-bodied *gringa* have formed this kind of a friendship over E-mail, of all things? I don't pretend to understand everything that needs to happen to take us to the next stage as multiculturalists. I think what we've teleographed, how we stayed stuck, how we imagine we might move through this time, are really just the tip of the iceberg. I don't want us to be too simplistic or naive about the work ahead of us, Jesse. In my heart I believe we will look back and find that we did the right things, we got unstuck, and we moved ahead. I already see the signs. What about you, my realistic (pessimistic?) friend?

Jesse: I'm waiting for the time when all us multiculturalists will make, respect, and appreciate each other heart-to-heart without being quite so concerned about all the presumptuous posing, grandstanding, and posturing. *Somos corderos y coyotes todos/* we are all lambs and coyotes, let's start from there. That's what worked for us, no?

Asian Indian Diaspora
Gargi Roysircar

The Color of Race

They stare at me as if I were
an eggplant among eggs,
a mango tree flourishing in a cornfield,
a Bengal Tigress grazing with Herefords.

See the frozen stares at the corner table—
those two farm boys with sludge to their knees,
that farmer in the Dekalb Feed cap?
Any moment now they'll be whispering through curled lips,
"forner," not believing my Americanness,
and seeing only my Indianness.

White friend, when you were in Calcutta, India,
children at the sight of your paleness
shouted "*shada chambra*,"—white skin—
and "*sahib*,"—white master—
ten thousand times a day,
market women cheated off your naïveté,
young men dogged you shop to shop
jostled at your elbow
and asked how tall you are.

Listen, you and I, my friend, see our race
through others' eyes.

Taxonomy of Privileged and Not Privileged

> I like this taxonomy of things.
> This clean delineation: In Calcutta
> you are a beggar, I am not.
> You are starving, I am not.
> We have our motives:
> yours is to stay alive,
> mine is to stay aloof, to avoid
> geometric proliferation.
> If I give you a rupee*
> you will become a hundred beggars.
> You know I couldn't give rupees
> to a hundred beggars.
> So I give none.
> You understand, don't you,
> I don't want to be unfair.

Note. An approximate analogy for this basic unit in Indian currency is what a dollar means to an American.

Killing in Religion's Name

Someone will always want something
he or she doesn't have.
Someone will always want to keep it.
Then in religion's name one will kill another.
And flesh of fathers will shatter,
seared skin of brothers,
all the broken sisters,
and the howling mouths of mobs;
trains will vomit their dead,
rivers shudder with Indira Gandhi's ashes
and India's agony.
Mother India, I mourn you,
but no less I mourn
the Golden Temple's cornered Sikhs,
the burned taxi drivers of New Delhi,
skewered Muslims in Calcutta,
slaughtered Hindus in Dhaka.
The Islamic bomb, the Hindu bomb,
Israeli-Palestinian zero-sum escalation,
no less here: Oklahoma City, Waco, Ruby Ridge, 9/11 jihads,
and all the miserable killers
all who kill
and will be killed, killed, killed.

On This Same Earth

There is a soothing comfort understanding
we all live on this same earth
whether in Keene, New Hampshire, or Calcutta, West Bengal
we see the same sky, sun, and stars.

When it's night in Keene
the sun shines in Calcutta,
But that's the way things are.
Rhododendrons bloom in spring
unknown to faraway Bengal.
But that's the way things are.
There are no summer monsoons here
which the farmer's rice fields welcome.
In New Hampshire, winter brings mounds of snow.
Even this difference doesn't matter.
There is a soothing comfort understanding
we all live on this same earth.

The Connecticut River freezes
cars get stuck on slopes
snow ploughs work the streets all night
school children next door don't go to school—
it's a snow day.
Naked trees in Robin Hood Park and up the hill
shiver with dreams of spring and new life.
No one here knows Grandmother's hand-sewn quilt
as I keep warm in an L.L. Bean down comforter.

Fog hangs low—
Suddenly Keene, its town center and penciled church steeple,
and Walgreen strip mall
look dimly like Calcutta, its Garia Hat bazaars with beautiful silk saris,
and Commilla, Father's Muslim birthplace.

Visible and invisible minority: Double-whammy or double blessing?

Luis A. Rivas

Visible Minority

I vividly remember many years ago leaving my homeland of Puerto Rico to pursue my collegiate education at Purdue University in West Lafayette, Indiana. I was not prepared for the cultural shock that I experienced. Growing up in Puerto Rico, everybody around me was the same. We all spoke the same language, celebrated the same holidays, shared the same traditions, held similar values and beliefs. While in college, the more I looked around me, the more I realized I was different from most other students at Purdue University, and from most other people in West Lafayette, Indiana.

These differences were thrown in my face before I was emotionally ready to deal with them. The first weekend I was at Purdue, even before classes had started, a Puerto Rican friend of mine was sexually assaulted. The reason the attacker gave her was "That's what Latin women are for." I attempted to support her in this process. However, a year after this incident she was no longer at Purdue. While it would be easy to attribute her leaving the university solely to this experience, the truth is that it only helped to color what her (and my) experience at Purdue was.

I had a hard time adjusting. I was used to friendliness and cooperation. At Purdue it seemed that everybody looked down as they walked, avoiding eye contact and interactions with you. My social group seemed to drift towards Puerto Rican students who shared similar experiences to mine. We tried to support each other as we learned about life in the United States. This was no easy task.

We were often reminded that we were different from others. People would sometimes come to us and tell us to talk in English, because "That's the language we speak in this country." This happened to me at the mall, in my dorm, at the bank, in fast food restaurants, and in different places around campus. As I think back about these incidents I can't help but laugh at how innocent my ignorance was. My immediate reaction to these comments used to be, "But I'm from Puerto Rico... We're part of this country too! And we don't speak English!" I attempted many different ways to fit in. For two years I was in the university's "All-American" marching band. I was the only

Hispanic student out of almost 400 people. I joined the Psychology club and was the only Hispanic student. I tried Big Brothers/Big Sisters, and once again I was the only one different. Even attending church seemed different. After my first brief confession I remember asking the priest, "That's it? We're done? Aren't you going to talk to me about my problems and how to be a better Catholic?"

After my freshman year I became involved in the "*Asociación de Hermanos Hispanos*" (Hispanic Brotherhood Association). This was a student organization that attempted to create the type of welcoming environment, so important to succeed academically, that we felt was missing at Purdue University. We shared a small office with the Chinese student organization. I remember sitting in the office one day and overhearing the Chinese students talk about a friend of theirs who needed reconstructive facial surgery because he was walking alone at night and somebody jumped off a pickup truck to beat him until he was unconscious.

As more of these types of incidents occurred I became more aware of my surroundings, I realized that I was now considered and seen by others as a "minority". This I learned carried a certain set of consequences. Pragmatically, I knew that there were certain places where I was not welcomed. I also knew better than to walk alone at night. Psychologically, I had some control over the way I came across to other people, but at times felt powerless about how other people perceived me. Sometimes they would have a preconceived notion of what I was like before they really got to know me. This would occasionally hinder my interactions with other people and my ability to be effectively understood by them.

Why did my classmates never include me in their study groups? Why did teaching assistants rarely call on me to participate in class discussions? How come the grading curve line was always drawn right above my social security number when grades were posted? I became painfully aware of what it is like to have other people judge you and form an impression of you without affording you an opportunity to prove yourself and explain what you are about. The dangers of seeing individuals as group members and attaching labels to them became very real to me.

Maybe these experiences are the reason why, since I began my advanced studies in psychology, I have never been able to comprehend the concept of a "mental disorder" or what the word "disorder" really means. As I understand it there is a common order that is agreed upon by everybody, and everything that deviates from it is referred to as a "disorder". But if that is the case, who gets to define what that common order is? What special qualities or qualifications must an individual have to be able to define another individual's experience and the extent to which they deviate from the norm? When I became a "minority", I certainly did not have a say over what that meant for me and how others were or were not to perceive me. Yet it affected, and still affects, my everyday life. No matter how many professional degrees I attain or how much good I may do in the world, people will still judge my character and me by the preconceived notions that they have of others who are like me. Nevertheless, not until I was diagnosed with Attention Deficit/Hyperactivity Disorder (ADHD) did these issues become the central aspects of my life.

Invisible Minority

It was quite an amazing and eye-opening experience undergoing an assessment and diagnosis process. In my opinion all psychologists should experience this as part of their training in interacting with people. Clinicians tend to underestimate the power that as counselors and psychologists we have over people. Being diagnosed with ADHD set in motion another very challenging process of learning about myself, not unlike the culture shock I first experienced coming to the United States.

My initial reaction was to discredit what this diagnosis meant. So I had ADHD… I was still the same person I was the week before. Nothing had really changed inside of me. Nevertheless, everything did change very quickly, as I decided to explore what Attention Deficit meant and why I supposedly had it. The first place I turned to was the DSM-IV, the *Diagnostic and Statistical Manual of Mental Disorders*. There, under the heading "Disorders first diagnosed during childhood" I found a few pages that did an outstanding job of describing what my life was like.

Soon after this experience everything started falling into place for me: "Diagnostic and Statistical Manual of Mental *Disorders*"… "*Disorders* first diagnosed during childhood"… "Attention Deficit/Hyperactivity *Disorder*". I was a "disordered" individual! That was why nobody else understood me when I talked about how hard it was for me to stop driving so fast all the time. That was why I was always the last one out whenever I would take tests in school. That was why I could never seem to return a book to the library without getting an overdue notice. I had a mental "disorder" and they did not! My

initial experience with the professional literature led to the development
of a negative image of myself that eventually took years to correct. I
then turned to my close friends and relatives for support. They all
responded with the same initial reaction when told about my ADHD:
"Big Deal!"... "So what?"... "You are still the same person that you
were the last time I talked to you". However, by this point my response
had dramatically shifted to: "But you don't understand! I have this
mental disorder! I have a learning disability."

The more I attempted to get support from others, the more I
felt my experience was being discredited and invalidated. With time
my self-esteem began to lessen, and I began defining myself by my
mental disorder. In doing this, I began doing to myself what others had
already being doing before in judging me by my "minority" status
rather than judging me as a person. I was then inflicting those negative
consequences of that behavior on myself.

As I continued to feel discounted and ignored by others'
reactions to my disclosures, I decided to seek the support that I need
within myself. I began to get more educated on Attention
Deficit/Hyperactivity Disorder, this time through the Internet and other
non-professional literature. It was then that I discovered I was not
really "disordered", and that there were many other individuals out
there who shared similar experiences to mine (including very eminent
and admirable people like Dustin Hoffman, Benjamin Franklin, Albert
Einstein, and Sylvester Stallone). I found out that as long as I let others
define my experience for me, I was always going to see myself the way
they saw me: "Disordered".

In obtaining a better understanding of my ADHD I began
integrating this aspect of me into my overall personal identity. ADHD
is a component of me, much like being of "minority" status here in the
United States is. Nevertheless, I feel that there is so much more to me
than what meets the eye. This is precisely the message that my initial
intuitive reaction first told me. It is also the same message that the
constant reactions of all my friends and relatives had attempted to
convey. With time, and lots of trials and tribulations, I had overcome
what felt like a scarlet letter thrust upon me by my mental "disorder"
diagnosis.

Double Whammy

My experience adjusting to life in the United States as a
"minority" mimics in many ways my experience coping with my
ADHD diagnosis. On both occasions I was forced to question my
identity and myself. Twice I was made to feel different. As a

"minority", I learned and internalized the fact that I was different from the normal "majority" around me. Reading the multicultural psychology literature on counseling Hispanic/Latino clients seemed to reduce my life experience to a handful of pages. As somebody with a "disorder", I learned and internalized the fact that I deviated from the normal order. Reading the DSM-IV description of Attention-Deficit/Hyperactivity Disorder also seemed to reduce my life experience to a handful of pages.

Interestingly (and sadly) enough, the field of psychology serves as a vivid example for the parallels present in these two statuses. My status as a "minority" individual has continuously been reinforced as I've continued to stay in school pursuing higher education. I chose to enter a field that is predominantly White, consistent with the "majority" status and the "majority" point of view. For example, all six of my graduate classmates were "majority" white students. The difference was very evident. I remember feeling extremely shocked the first time I was referred to by a professor as a "person of color". "Don't we all have color?" I thought.

Soon after beginning graduate school I attended my first American Psychological Association (APA) regional conference. I was looking forward to meeting other Spanish-speaking students who I could share my experiences with. What I found was very disheartening. Not only was I the only Hispanic student, but there were only 2 other "minority" black students.

My experience in the classroom was not very validating either. Most of the research, theories, and clinical interventions that I have been taught and exposed to in my training have been based on a traditional Western approach. For example, learning about the different "objective" instruments in my assessment class was always an interesting experience. The questions in the Minnesota Multiphasic Personality Inventory - 2 (MMPI-2) were very difficult for me to understand and answer. "I do not read every editorial in the newspaper every day" - well, when I am in Puerto Rico I do. I only spend two weeks there every year and I try to catch up with the issues facing the country as best I can. However, when I am in the United States I do not. "I have strong political opinions" - once again, when I am in Puerto Rico I do. I, as most Puerto Ricans, feel very passionately about my country. However, when I am in the United States I do not get involved in U.S. politics. I took several other psychological instruments as part of the class, and I often scored in the clinically significant range. Taking the Wechsler Adult Intelligence Scale - Revised (WAIS-R) was also another adventure. "Where does the sun rise" - well, when I was growing up living by the sea I used to see it come over the ocean every morning. Is that the answer you want? "What is the population of the United States?" - I don't know, but I can tell you how many people live in Puerto Rico.

My status as a "disordered" individual has also seemingly been reinforced as I've continued to pursue my training in this field. It is simply amazing to notice the reactions that others have when I disclose this aspect of my identity. How ironic: a psychotherapist with a "mental disorder". There is nothing that will disturb and confuse a psychotherapist more than to hear another psychotherapist or coworker say, "I haven't been feeling myself today because I forgot to take my medication this morning".

The manner in which different people process that statement is very telling of the way they perceive and experience me. Sometimes, my colleagues will look at me as if there is something "wrong" or "defective" because of my ADHD. Others, usually support or secretarial staff (i.e., those *not* trained in counseling and psychotherapy) are more open to understanding what my experience is and are less likely to readily assign a set of personality traits and characteristics to me. Overall, my status as an individual different from those around me is very quickly highlighted and validated.

I sometimes feel jealous of those who have not lived through the experiences that I have lived through. I can't help but be aware that, in questioning my normalcy and the extent to which I am or am not different from everybody else, I have not led a "normal" life. To this day, it is still very hard for me to wonder whether I was treated a certain way because of something I did or because of the way somebody else perceived me.

Double Blessing

These last nine years since I came to the United States have been an absolute struggle for me, in more ways than one. I have continuously been forced to question who I am, and have constantly struggled to develop a personal identity. I have also had to deal with adjusting to the manner in which other people perceive and judge my behavior and me as a person, something that I often do not have any control of. In a way it's as if some of that childhood innocence and ignorance that I experienced growing up in Puerto Rico as a "majority" individual has been taken away from me.

I previously stated feeling jealous at those who have not experienced the struggles that I have had to deal with. Nevertheless, I feel that I have reached the point in my life when I can honestly say I would not trade these hard and sometimes very painful experiences for a more "normal" life. These experiences have shaped the person that I am today, and have also shaped the way I process what goes on around me in this sometimes very harsh society.

When I started graduate school I was homophobic. I had never taken the time to stop and think about why I made fun of people who were homosexuals. I just did. Nevertheless, the continuous development of my identity as a 'minority' facilitated the exploration of my homophobic attitudes and behavior. I remember talking one night with a friend of mine, who happened to be gay, about our collegial relationship. I told him, "When I see you as a gay person first, I am doing the very same thing that other people who see me as a 'minority' do to me." This conversation triggered an evolving scrutinized look at the validity of my homophobic beliefs. Being in touch with my experiences as a "minority" constantly challenges how I perceive other people and the extent to which I am imposing my own set of values on them.

Clients have occasionally told me during sessions: "I don't want you to think I'm depressed or manic because I don't want you to think I'm crazy". To which I will often reply, "As a minority here in the United States I know what it's like to be judged without being given an opportunity to express myself. You can feel confident that I will not do that to you." Coming to terms with the different experiences I have encountered through the years has allowed me to better understand whom I am and what I have to offer others. I am also better able to treat clients as human beings first, and whatever labels or diagnoses they may carry with them second.

Whether it is race, gender, sexual orientation, or simply the status that being a psychologist carries in your church, community, or extended family, we have all experienced situations in which we are identified as 'minority' individuals. If we can get past the positive and negative connotations that these labels bring, we can begin to understand what it is like to be perceived as different. The extent to which we have tackled these opportunities, whether by choice or necessity, has influenced the way we perceive ourselves and the image we project to others.

Conclusion

It has been my intention with this personal narrative to shed light into some of the internal processes and struggles that go on in adjusting to labels, in this case "minority" and "mental disorder". I hope the reader is more aware of the potential consequences that come

with classifying somebody according to how she or he perceives that individual. While we all rely on categories and labels as a way to structure and order our world, it is important to realize that this action does not come without consequences.

I do not feel completely comfortable labeling the experiences that I have described above as "unfair". They were part of my life, and life is not always fair. Nevertheless, I do feel the need to emphasize the potentially detrimental consequences that come with defining other people's experiences for them. In labeling other individuals and treating them according to whatever perception you have of them, you are creating an environment that predisposes the person to experience these feelings.

Individuals are often treated according to how they are perceived. Individuals will often act in a manner consistent with others' perceptions of them. It was my experience that when I allowed others' perceptions to color my own existence and perception of myself, my experience became whatever other people wanted it to be. However, the more I defined myself and controlled who I was, my experience - and my life - became my own.

My Barn Having Burned to the Ground, I Can Now See the Moon
Michael Murphy

In December of 1998 I was seriously depressed. Clinically depressed. Diagnosable. That's not easy for me to admit. I'm a therapist. My job is to help people who are depressed – not to *be* depressed.

Alexander Lowen, the brilliant Bioenergetic therapist, writes that depression is the inevitable result of illusion giving way to reality. Marion Woodman, a Jungian analyst, calls depression the inevitable result of the collapse of our addiction to perfection. We therapists are supposed to be perfect aren't we? Many (Most?) of us go into this work to be the savior … and often to further bury our neuroses. Most of us deny our perfectionist strivings – even though they are so easily recognized by our colleagues (and clients) nonetheless. As my colleague and friend one time said (at a staff retreat): "it's hard working with perfect people". We all laughed but his honesty cut to the heart of many of the staff's dynamics and individual struggles.

I too thought I had shed the last of my perfectionism. I had changed a lot in my 18 years as a therapist. Much less neurotic and savior-like. But in November I was to learn a deeper lesson about my issues. In November a family "crisis" happened. One of my beloved sons dove head-first into a very difficult time.

I should say something here about how I value my two sons. I have always been clear that parenting is my primary "job" in this lifetime. Far more important than my career and professional life. When my first son was born I have never felt such joy. And again with my second. I love my partner very much but the love I have/had for my sons is different … it's like they are a piece of me. A writer friend of mine once said: "watching your child make her/his way in the world is like watching your heart walk around outside your body." So lovely, so alive ... and *so* vulnerable! And so it seemed to me. When making those difficult choices between going to one of my son's elementary school plays or going to a professional meeting or responsibility I *always* chose the former. I had seen too many fathers miss these moments in their children's lives. I was clear that I would not be one of those dads. I reveled in the role of father – hopefully not in an egotistical, overindulgent way ... rather simply as a father who knew his priorities and chose to live accordingly. And the connection I felt (feel) with my sons was (is) intense. So when my oldest son's life (and ours at the same time) turned upside down it was very painful.

My first response was to do everything a good (perfect) parent (and therapist) should do to help him right the ship. But after a few weeks it became clear that everything I/we did only made matters worse. Slowly it dawned on me that there was little I could do to control the situation. All my well-honed therapy skills didn't help.

After a few weeks of being an ineffective parent I plunged into depression. First an anxious, frantic sort of depression – then a crushing, gut-wrenching depression. I couldn't sleep, I lost my appetite, and I didn't want to go to work. I hated being with clients and I despised being with colleagues. This was *so* strange for me ... I had always *loved* going to work. Now being with clients was a chore. I didn't want to hear their problems. During sessions I thought mainly of my own problems and of my son's struggle. I was agitated, jumpy, and inattentive. I didn't dare go near painful emotions with my clients – mine were far too near the surface and in constant danger of erupting. I struggled to control and cover up my own anxiety.

I avoided colleagues like the plague. I found reasons to miss meetings. And when I did attend I was only about 20% present. I avoided my colleagues (many of whom were also my friends) for fear of them seeing how depressed I was. To this day I still don't know how many of them knew the depth of my struggle – the degree of how deeply I was "handicapped" professionally. I still find it rather strange that only one of them (a very dear friend) openly approached me about my struggle.

To be fair, I am a master at hiding my pain. I developed this survival "skill" in my family. There was no room for display of pain there. I mastered this skill and it has both served me well and handicapped me throughout my life. So, of course, in crisis I reverted to my hiding behavior. Did I really fool all of my colleagues? Probably not. Then why didn't they say something? During my crisis I *prayed* that they wouldn't notice - that they wouldn't ask me. But later, crisis resolved, I marveled at how people so sensitive and caring could *not* notice – or not inquire. People who inquire many times each day about their clients' pain – and yet they never inquired about mine. Professional courtesy? A trust in my strength of character? Not wanting to pry? All of these I suppose. And yet I still find myself wondering. It reminds me of a haunting experience of many years ago.

In a rare intimate senior staff gathering one older male staff member broke down and cried as he told of a former counselor at our Center who had committed suicide. Apparently people had known she was feeling "down". But her death was a shock. That one conversation is the only time in 15 years I have ever heard this even mentioned. Ashamed? Protective? I don't know. But I do know that when I was depressed that it felt very strange to have no one "notice".

During that time I continued with my clients, and my supervision of graduate students, and my meetings - but I operated in a fog for about a month. My supervision was awful, my therapy only slightly better. I struggled just to make it through each hour.

I sat in this bone-crushing depression for about six weeks. I re-entered therapy but it didn't help. I tried a new therapist – he had all the solutions (or so he said). That didn't help either. We did family therapy – no help. Finally I entered therapy with another person – an older, very wise person who challenged me to confront my powerlessness and control issues.   He confronted me with my helplessness and the reality of the situation (i.e., I was doing everything I could do and still the situation with my son was getting "worse"). I hated this! I didn't want to face my limited ability to control/help my son. My therapist forced me to. No easy answers. Just the deep pain of facing reality just as it was.

Later in describing why this therapy was different (from previous therapy) I said to a friend, "I finally found a therapist I couldn't charm." This was so important. He was kind and supportive but he spared me no pain. He created no illusions and he did not collude with my creating illusions. And eventually I learned to tolerate the pain and to trust all of me - even the part that couldn't "save" my son - and the part that was helpless and "ineffective".

My therapist also encouraged me to deal with the unresolved trauma from my childhood. Having done a lot of my own therapy over the years I was sure I had resolved this trauma. But I was wrong. Just as our clients are wrong when they insist that those old family issues are "no longer a problem." I didn't want to face these issues. I didn't want to admit the deep pain I had at not being able to save my mother from her life of despair. That I couldn't "save" my family from its incredible chaos and unhappiness. Like so many therapists, I was the hero child. The one supposedly unaffected (or *least* affected) by my family's struggles: my mom's debilitating depression and suicide attempts; my parents' desperate unhappiness, with each other, themselves, and life in general; of my sisters' hush-hush teenage pregnancy, sexual abuse, and drug addiction. Through it all I achieved. Unaffected. A sports star in junior high and high school (lettering in basketball, baseball and golf, nearly making first team all-state in basketball), a college graduate, and then a Ph.D.! And yet despite all the "success" and achievement I couldn't save my mom or my family. And now I couldn't save my son.

Slowly, gradually, after a couple months of therapy my depression began to lift. Not rapidly, but slowly - like snow melts in spring. My therapy forced me to confront my demons, one by one. It forced me to re-examine, process, and grieve my childhood losses and issues. I once described to a friend my recovery feeling much like it feels to go through the death of a beloved family member. Anger, denial, bargaining, and finally acceptance and relief. But slowly. Grief work of the deepest kind. Grieving the loss of my illusion, the illusion of what I thought my (and my son's) life would be.

Ever so slowly I began to see the gift that this crisis had brought. Early in the crisis a friend and colleague gave me a very poignant and prophetic card. It said simply: "my barn having burned to the ground, I can now see the moon." As I recovered, that is exactly what it began to feel like. I now truly understand what the mystics call "the dark night of the soul". Where we question our very basic assumptions and images of ourselves and life.

I came to realize how I had been using psychology to hide. If only I got enough degrees, enough credentials - maybe I wouldn't have to face the pain in my own life. Maybe I could be infallible - immune to suffering and pain. Or at least I would know how to deal with it in a rational, elegant manner. But just like our clients, I needed a "dark night" to help me face it directly and resolve it. There was no place to hide.

In time I came to truly recognize the "hidden gift" in such deep, dark depression. I was forced to look at my deepest issues. And coming through this "dark night" I found incredible strength. I felt stronger than I had ever felt in my life. After the depression lifted I found myself *being* with clients (and friends) in new ways. I was more present; less anxious; less fearful; more open and vulnerable; more imperfect; more "out there". I spoke my mind more easily. I cared less what clients (and other people) thought of me. I found myself appreciating their struggles in a new way. Very able to be with them in their pain. Their pain no longer scared me. I had been there - and come back. I am now acutely aware of how many of us (psychologists/therapist) try to avoid our pain, but of course in doing so we also miss the lesson. I was now able to be with clients and their deep pain, their "dark night", in a different way. A deeper, calmer way. I used to tell clients that going through "the dark night of the soul" was necessary. Necessary pain. Necessary to their discovering their true selves. I feel a bit foolish now for telling them this before having gone through it myself. Or perhaps not foolish, just so much wiser now myself for having gone through it. Did it make me perfect? No way! Imperfect? Fallible? Vulnerable? Definitely. It "broke open" my heart and at least some of its armor melted. My heart opened more to life - the pain and the joy.

I can now look back and thank my son for plunging me into the abyss. When I was in the abyss I never imagined that I would be thankful to him. But I am. Perhaps such deep pain is truly the only way we learn about the "darker" parts of our true selves. In my view, much of psychology training serves to more deeply bury our pain. Then later, we further bury our pain in our professional competency issues. Like piling more earth on top of a rich archeological dig. To find the "real stuff" we must dig deep. That cannot be accomplished intellectually. It is only through deep emotional pain that such unearthing occurs.

I'm certain that I have many more lessons to learn in this lifetime. And I'm sure some of them will be very painful. I used to think, not rationally but at a deep, unconscious level, that I was immune to such pain. If I was a good enough person, or a good enough psychologist, I could control my life enough to (largely) avoid such deep pain. Now I know that is not true. And, strangely, I'm glad it's not true. This crisis, this dark night of my soul, has given me more life - not less.

Thank you, son, for making me a more complete person and therapist. I am deeply indebted to you - and so are my clients.

Out of Our Control
Anonymous

The minutes dragged as I waited for my wife, Ann, and my thirteen-year-old son, Jeff, to emerge from the supermarket. I was steaming, not just because it was August, but because Ann often kept me waiting. We'd fought over this problem so many times that I'd given up trying to change her. When they arrived, I thought, I would quickly let her know that I didn't appreciate being disrespected, and then do my best to forget about the whole thing. However, since lateness is Ann's worst fault, I'm still convinced that I was lucky enough to marry the pick of the litter. Tick, Sweat, Tock, Grrr, Tick, Sweat, Tock, C'mon, Tick, Sweat, Tock, Where are they? Tick, Grrr, Tock, Sweat, Tick . . . You know the feelings.

Finally, I could take it no longer. I stormed into the supermarket to get them to move their sorry butts. I searched the entire store, but they were nowhere. Returning to my car, concern began to replace anger. By the time I went back into the supermarket, fear had completely displaced my anger. Ann and Jeff were in a checkout line with three items in their shopping cart. Their faces seemed to have aged years in less than an hour.

"What's wrong?"

"Jeff was caught shoplifting."

Jeff??!! Our perfect son, Jeff!!?? There must be some mis . . .

Sitting on our bed, Ann and I asked Jeff to explain what had happened. He didn't know what happened. Wandering the aisles, he had put a Right Guard deodorant stick and three Binaca breath sprays in his pocket. When he got to the check out line, he placed the Right Guard in the shopping cart. However, Jeff said that he knew that his mother wouldn't buy the Binacas. So the contraband breath sprays remained in his pocket. Jeff reported that he had no idea why he did it, and he swore on a stack of Bibles that he had never before stolen anything. I breathed a deep sigh of relief as I reflected upon Jeff's spotless record for honesty.

Upon being liberated from our inquisition, Jeff headed straight out the front door. "Do you think he's looking for Paul and Harry?" Ann asked. Of course he was! They had been inseparable ever since Harry had moved into the neighborhood three months earlier.

Suddenly, three Binacas had an ominous feel. "Get him back here," Ann ordered.

Jeff and Paul had only exchanged a few sentences when I arrived. I escorted Jeff home, and then returned to Paul's house. No parents were home, so I asked Paul if he would mind answering some questions, or would he prefer to wait until I obtained his father's permission. "No problem," he replied. I told Paul that I knew about the stealing, and that I wanted to hear the whole story from him. Yes, he admitted, they had stolen sunglasses from a store in the mall.

"Who was there?" I asked

"The three of us," Paul replied.

"Who took the glasses?"

"All three of us."

"Three pairs of glasses?"

"Yes."

"When was this?"

"A little over a week ago."

Perhaps it was the thunderstruck look on my face, or perhaps he realized that I was asking a lot of very basic questions for a guy who supposedly knew everything, but Paul suddenly shifted into a soliloquy. He began detailing how this was the only time they had ever stolen anything, how sorry they were, how wrong they knew it was to steal, and why we could be certain they would never steal again. Then he swore the veracity of all that he said on the same stack of Bibles that Jeff had just desecrated. I sent Paul home and headed straight for Harry's house.

When I mentioned stealing to Harry's father, he was not completely surprised. Harry's peers were an important reason for their recent move to our neighborhood. Wishing me well, Harry's dad urged me to find out all I could from Harry before the three sets of parents caucused to determine how to proceed.

"Harry, I know all about the stealing. The only thing at stake here is whether, when we're finished, I say to your dad, 'He told me everything' or 'Sorry, Harry is still covering up.'"

I thought I had all the relevant facts until Harry told me of five other shoplifting episodes that the three had engineered over the last few weeks. How could things have deteriorated so far so fast?

The group of parents met alone. Each of the boys' parents met with their child separately. We obtained manuals on stealing and made each of the boys write extensively about their thoughts, feelings, and actions. Each family reviewed the written materials with their child. The boys and their parents met as a large group. A therapist was hired to provide weekly group therapy sessions for the boys. We met with officials from the local probation department. We apologized and made restitution to all of the merchants involved. We grounded the boys for some time. We attended a four-week program on shoplifting at the local probation office. We tried everything we could possibly imagine, and we still don't feel good.

Ann and I have tried to understand the hollow feelings in our stomachs, but no analysis seems compelling. Had we raised Jeff badly? We could see no other signs of bad parenting. Was this simply the first instance of what will become ongoing adolescent conduct problems? Oh God, we hope not. Was our good little boy simply led astray by bad peers? The other two boys seem just as good as Jeff, it seems they were all guilty of pressuring one another. Then what went wrong? Frankly, I don't know.

Fear and not knowing what went wrong are the causes of the hollow feeling in my stomach. How can I be confident that I'm now doing a better job, if I still don't know what went wrong the first time? I put a lot of trust in the boys. Or did I just find it convenient to not check up on much of what they said and did? I had naively thought I could protect Jeff from most sources of harm in this world. I now know that was my fantasy, as any teen can easily land in jail.

What really bothered me was how bad the boys had been as friends to one another. They supported and even goaded each other to do things that would harm all of them. They didn't even want most of the junk they stole! It was there. It seemed easy to steal and they believed they wouldn't get caught. Each didn't want to fall behind the theft rate of the others—it was a stupid contest! Each had been abysmally bad at resisting the peer pressures of the other two. Even at this late date, none of them has mentioned that their actions were morally wrong.

What's a father to do? I still believe we've done a good job raising Jeff. I am convinced he is a wonderful boy. I know that every crisis represents an opportunity, and I can already see Jeff growing from this experience. His adolescent sense of omnipotence has taken quite a hit. Good! He has had a painful taste of why he sometimes needs to fight peer pressure tooth-and-nail. Fantastic! He'll need all the strength he can get because he has yet to confront drugs, cars, cheating, gangs, sex, and on and on.

But I still haven't identified the source of the fear that constantly churns in my stomach — that black hole that now devours every shred of confidence I try to manufacture to allay my fears. The truth is that I now know that Jeff's safety is quickly slipping out of my control. He could have been thrown into the juvenile detention center—and we all know what happens to good boys in there. I would have been powerless to stop it. He is growing away from me. He already lied to me to protect his peers. I don't want him to ruin his life, and I fear I can never again be completely at ease, knowing that I don't know all that he is thinking. And finally, I worry that he is growing up in an unsafe world. Ours is a world where kids are routinely misled, blindsided, and then written-off. I'd feel a little better if I believed his friends would help him to make good decisions, but that hope rings hollow for me right now—as I'm certain it must for Paul's and Harry's parents also.

It's been a rough summer. I'm glad we're all going back to school. We'll have lots of time to reflect upon what happened and how we'll allow it to shape our lives. I still think Jeff, Harry, and Paul are good boys. I hope this brush with danger will awaken them to the fact that if they don't watch out for themselves and one another, they'll bear the consequences of their actions. We parents can't protect them anymore. Their lives are now largely out of our control. Time will tell the tale of how wisely they chart the courses of their lives. Good luck, guys. And if there is any way I can be of help to you in your decisions, please, please, please ask for my help—if you can.

Changing the Default Mode in the Hard Drive of Life
Cindy Anderson Keene

I know I will need to call the police again when a well-worn tennis shoe aimed for my head bashes another hole in the white wall of our family room. He gallops toward me and I dodge into the bedroom forcing the door closed behind me. But like many of the other doors in our home, the lock is broken; indeed a gaping hole is left behind. The brass knob and lock lay in pieces on the windowsill, a screwdriver along side, Barrett's attempt to put the pieces back together again. I race for the phone and punch in the three rescue numbers before he grabs it away, boxing my ear in the maneuver. Did I make a connection? If so they will call back immediately, even drive over if they do not get a response.

"Did you call the police?"

"Yes."

"Stupid idiot. It won't do any good." He rips the telephone cord from the wall. "I hung it up before they answered." He spits profane insults that assault my consciousness and shatter my heart, incomprehensible epithets, given their source.

Barrett posts himself in front of the door clutching the phone in one hand, his other hand a fist that opens and closes over and over. Behind me is a window wall looking out on a lakeside forest. Green feathery branches of giant old hemlocks swoop down like gentle arms beckoning to lift me out, up, and away to a blue sky with puffy white clouds to hide in. Morning doves coo mournful love songs that drift in through the open window with fresh damp smells of spring. I stand at attention, facing him, my eyes riveted to the phone.

"Please let me leave." I modulate my tone of voice, careful not to whine or beg.

"Why?" He shrugs his shoulders and tosses his head.

"I have to go to the bathroom."

"Are you going to call the police?" He coughs and grimaces.

"I have to."

"No you don't."

"You know I do."

He hurls a glass against the wall, the shattered pieces

grinding, tinkling as they fall to the floor, crystal shards bouncing up around our ankles, prickling without piercing the skin. He looks surprised, yet proud that he has scared me and somehow won.

"Open the door." I demand it.

His face crumbles and he begins to cry, sobbing, pleading with me. "I'll clean it up, I'll fix the wall, I promise. I'll do anything you ask me to do. I love you."

"Give me the phone."

He lunges at me and I drop back onto the bed, cowering. His fist comes down on my back. It hurts, but I am okay; still I cry, softly at first, then sobbing.

"Why are you crying? You're not really crying, you're faking it." He leans over me and I smell his sweat, surprisingly fresh, yet his hair is greasy, in need of a shampoo. "What's wrong? What's wrong? Stop crying."

"I don't know what will become of you."

"Shut up."

I wish the phone would ring. I don't believe he would ever really hurt me but I'm afraid and suddenly exhausted, as though we've been battling like this all day. I feel like a hostage and just want this to be over with.

"Please let me go to the bathroom. I promise I won't call." I immediately regret this desperate lie.

He lets me escape upstairs to use the bathroom. The living room windows reveal an ancient oak, its massive trunk almost two stories high. The white walls have a soft rose tint, a backdrop for classical poster art, ornate gilded frames drawn around Victorian gowned women leisurely reading and looking out to sea. In a portrayal of Pygmalion, a sculptor gazes at his white plaster statue as it transforms itself into a real woman. In another painting, a young man and woman wearing transparent Grecian robes flee an advancing storm. A blonde Story & Clark piano, circa 1960, stands in the corner of the room. Flowery chintz upholstery adorns over-stuffed furniture. Polished oak floors run along the long hallway and foyer where a blue antique rice pot a top a glass table sprouts white statice. Potpourri smells of rose and lavender. A gray patch tabby cat sprawls on the floor dozing.

I hear a phone ring while in the bathroom and Barrett softly telling the caller that everything is okay, goodbye. He pounds out the opening scales of Beethoven's fifth symphony on the piano, loud, angry, primitive noises. He has talent but will not take lessons or learn to read notes, instead he punches out laborious repetitions of familiar melodies until they are just right, or he makes up a chaotic piece of his own.

I quietly steal to the garage, to my car, hoping he has forgotten about the cell phone. Locking myself in, I call 911. They had not received my earlier call and will send a squad car over right away. I wait for a while, not sure what to do next, and then go inside to tell Barrett.

"The police are on their way over."

"That was stupid. They can't do anything." He squeezes his eyes shut tight then wide open, then again two more times. "I hope you die of gonorrhea and rot in hell."

He stands to face me. He is my height now, but much broader. Blue eyes and dark blonde hair styled in a bowl cut reflect my image, reminiscent of me at his age. Freckles dot his nose, a few pimples. He is wearing a khaki T-shirt with white piping across the chest and a pair of baggy corduroy pants of which he has a least fifteen identical pairs in various colors. I know that underneath he is wearing both boxers and shorts. His shoes are well-worn, round-toed, blue suede Van's. Twelve going on thirteen, a boy sometimes a man.

I, as his mother, reach down into the deepest part of my spirit to marshal all the will and strength I possess to try to dig out and nourish the kind, gentle character who lives inside at the core of my son.

Like Barrett, I too regressed into attacks of rage on various occasions throughout my life, usually the result of a stew of circumstances, actions, people, frustrations, and exhaustion. But unlike Barrett, they were rare, and I did not swear profusely, twitch uncontrollably, or tic at all. Unlike Barrett, I did not have Tourette's syndrome. Apparently, I am a carrier of the Tourette's gene, which manifests itself in ubiquitous extended family dysfunction including obesity, alcoholism, depression, and divorce. "An emotional flurry of family events," a doctor once called it. I have suffered the latter two symptoms and other family members both the former and the latter. Barrett exhibits the more common Tourette's symptoms: facial and vocal tics, attention deficit hyperactivity, obsessive-compulsive behavior, oppositional defiance, attacks of rage, and profanity as a second language.

Our genetic makeup forms a foundation for the ways in which we act and ultimately play out our lives, but we possess a free will that allows us to make choices that direct our destiny. Why then, have I repetitiously made the wrong choices in my life just as Barrett does? It's as though the hard drive of my computer brain keeps shifting back to the default mode no matter how often I try to override it. I need to keep rereading the manual of life that provides the instructions to reprogram our genetic makeup. But it is hard text to follow, full of meaningless direction and lacking in explicitness. With each flying object and profane pronouncement Barrett hurls, I ask myself whether he is ticcing, Tourette's style, mimicking a caricature of his father, or playing out the anger and frustrations over the life and death of his parent's chaotic relationship. The answer to this mystery drives my daily search for truth.

My relationship with Barrett, unless I consciously override automatic tendencies, is often too familiar, reminiscent of historic battles with other loved ones. I search back in time, reliving my childhood, searching for the key of events that opens the secret chest of clues to Barrett's behavior. My history, my genetic makeup is the earth from which he germinated and thrived. And so I scrape at the topsoil of my life to expose the roots that feed the tree of our existence together.

Inside Barrett's head, trying to see the world through the eyes of this child, I recall my own mother. Most often, I found her lying on the couch or in bed under a white chenille bedspread of soft cotton that sprouted tufts of loopy cord. Her head enshrouded in pin curls, bobby pin crosses nailed circles of brown hair to her scalp. I don't think she was sick, nor sexy, boozy, or lazy. Bed was just where she seemed to like spending most of her time.

At times, though, she arose from a nap in a merry mood. "Let's make peanut butter fudge," she would offer. She'd boil brown sugar and water, and then drop small teaspoons of the goo into a measuring cup of cold water until it was at the "soft ball stage." Then she'd pour it all in a large blue mixing bowl, add a cup of chunky peanut butter and beat vigorously, her flowered cotton house dress swaying, black and white saddle shoes planted firmly to the floor. Then she'd scoop and scrape the steamy brown melange smelling of fresh roasted peanuts into a buttered glass pie plate where we stared at it, our mouths watering, until it was cool enough to eat.

Like Barrett, she also displayed fits of rage, manifested by fierce articulate lectures delivered to my sisters and me for various misdeeds of which we were judged guilty without fair representation or an accounting of the facts.

"I want to talk to you," was a dire warning.

I had to sit on one twin bed facing her while she sat on the other, pointing her finger, her face screwed up like a prune, eyebrows moving wickedly.

"You're a naughty girl; you ought to be ashamed of yourself. You deserve a spanking for this." No protestations of mine could keep her from bending me over her knee and whacking my behind with her flat, open hand. When I acted particularly naughty, she pulled down my pants so that the slapping smarted and made loud smacking sounds. I learned to believe that I was indeed an inconsiderate and malicious girl, the sole cause of my mother's pervasive unhappiness; I was guilty even of things I was unaware of having done.

"She's mean to me. She said I was bad when I wasn't," I often told my father. He listened grim-faced while I sat on his lap, one of his arms around me, the other hand running circles on my back.

"You must understand your mother. She doesn't feel well right now. She does a lot for you children and loves you very much. She doesn't mean to hurt you." He spoke in a low hush, his breath the familiar comforting smell of a loved one. "Now go do something nice for her, set the table for dinner."

I recall my father most often in the pulpit dressed in a long black cotton robe covered by a white satin tunic, a heavy gold cross hanging from a black cord around the clerical collar at his neck, delivering passionate contemporary sermons that tied the teachings of Christ into our everyday motives and actions. I grew up in the church, singing in the choir, attending Sunday school, summer vacation Bible School, weekday Bible School, confirmation classes, and Luther League. Church bestowed on me the gift of music. I marched, sang, and dreamily listened to the adult choir's complicated harmonizing spiced by a blonde, blue-eyed, soprano whose solos implored passionate pleas and praises to God. The liturgy mesmerized me as I sang the same words Sunday after Sunday, not needing to open the hymnal for as far back as I can remember. But the words coagulated the image of me that was already baking at home. "I am a sinner for I have sinned against thee in thought, word, and deed and only through your forgiveness and mercy will I attain everlasting life." Pictures of Christ hanging from the cross, his head bowed, dripping blood from a crown of thorns and nails in his hands and feet, reminded me that I had made Him suffer for my sins.

Political, ethnic and racial tension stressed the Milwaukee neighborhood where I grew up during the post World War II cold war era, though I was unaware of the etiology of the subtle apprehensions of the grown-up world. The city was founded by European immigrants, mostly German, the heritage of my own parents. My two best friends were Jewish, and even though one lived next door and the other just down the block, their parents sent them to a different elementary school because there were few Jewish children in the district school I attended. I was welcomed into their homes, though at times left with unaccountable feelings of alienation. No one talked about the Holocaust back then.

We had few toys growing up. My paternal grandmother gave me a chubby rubber doll that looked remarkable like a real baby for my fourth Christmas. Her visit from Minneapolis via rail that Christmas of 1955 ended tragically soon after the New Year. Sitting on my mother's lap the morning after Christmas, her protruding abdomen swollen with child, she put my shoes and socks on while I dressed my own baby doll. She was startled when we heard and felt a boom, not unlike the sonic booms we heard several years latter.

"It's Granny Ethel, she's fallen." We found Granny E on the floor of my sister's bedroom where she'd slept the night before. Dazed, apologetic, she claimed she was okay, but she was telling a lie.

That evening I cowered in a corner of the stairway landing while men in white coats carried Granny E out of my house and my life on a stretcher to an awaiting ambulance. Still in her fifties, she died young by today's standards, the result of poorly managed high blood pressure. Her divorce from my grandfather had been a hardship, one, I speculate, from which she never fully recovered. Whether her blood pressure was mismanaged by her or by the medical establishment remains a mystery. Also a quandary is how the medication to treat high blood pressure, which both my father and sister take for hypertension, are the drugs of choice for Barrett's Tourette symptoms and my migraine headaches.

I learned a shocking preschool lesson when my mother gave birth to my younger sister within weeks of my grandmother's death: With death comes life and the cycle repeats itself. I will give birth and I will die.

We didn't have Barbie dolls when I was growing up. When I wasn't an imaginary ballerina dancing pirouettes to the tune of Swan Lake in our living room, I raced the boys on our block down the ally, on foot or on a little fat-wheeled Schwinn bicycle. I took piano lessons The Melody Way, and was one of only two students at the Thirty-eighth Street School at that time to complete all 12 sessions. Without the encouragement to continue after my final recital, I never played the piano again. Nor did I sing again for the same reason.

Racial tensions boiled over into rioting in Milwaukee the summer of 1967 and my family coincidentally moved to a predominantly Christian, white middle-class suburb. A junior in high school, I did not fit into the cliques that had formed long before I arrived. I found solace in a relationship with a John Travolta look alike at a Saturday night dance. We necked and drank and raced around in his new shiny blue Dodge 440 RT racecar for which he pumped gas and washed cars forty hours a week to purchase and maintain.

My mother and I battled constantly over Richard Nixon, the Viet Nam War, the length of my dresses and the color of my hair, the hours of my appearance and disappearance and my newfound freedom and individuality. Her lectures continued, with different titles, but the same theme and message. I was guilty, shameful, inconsiderate, irresponsible, tactless, irreverent, a disappointment and the cause of her unhappiness and embarrassment. My reactions to them changed during my adolescence. I vengefully threw back at her the same accusations and incriminations, the same guilt inducing mantras that came from her lips.

I went away to college with my John Travolta in 1969. We rented a farmhouse in the country, where we grew vegetables, chickens, marijuana, and long hair. (My father grew gray hair, my mother a bouffant). We married; I received a Bachelor's Degree, became a social worker, and started graduate school. He liked to abuse alcohol and other drugs, rarely came home for dinner, if at all, and left orange peels on the arm of the sofa in neat little cup-like piles.

I celebrated my twenty-third birthday with a male classmate, a kind, vivacious New York Italian who informed me for the first time in my life that I was not just attractive, but intelligent as well. It suddenly struck me, as though I'd been the tin man all this time - without emotional capacity, that I abhorred my husband.

"I want to move out," I told him.

"Then go." Angry and wounded, his balled fists flexed the well-developed muscles in his arms and chest until they bulged through his T-shirt. He grabbed me by the arm and hurled me toward the door. I ran, returning when I knew it was safe to load up my red VW Bug with everything I could possibly need to live on my own.

Fully aware at the time that I had married a jerk who used and abused me, and that I'd found someone who would treasure and respect me, I nevertheless seemed compelled to fall back into a default mode of fighting old battles with a mother figure. It seemed that a contentious relationship was programmed into my hard drive of a brain. My mother figure came in the form of a powerful, highly successful, seductive surgeon eight years my senior. I tearfully said good-bye to the New York Italian, embarking on an unforeseen journey back to the future. I naively hoped to transform the seductive surgeon, teach him love, acceptance, and trust. I gave him these gifts, which he greedily devoured but did not return in kind.

By moonlight, I arose a goddess, beautiful, brilliant, and profound. In the black of night I grew stupid, a failure, lazy, unworthy. During the light of day, I did not exist at all. Such is the reflection in the mirror held by one who drinks. I thrived on the moonlight, went to bed early, and ran with the morning sun.

Still, we married, had two children, and built a large home. I coped with his alcoholic mood swings the same way I coped with my mother's dichotomous personality. I escaped into running, biking, and learning, playing house and caring for my babies. I went back to school, studied to be as smart as he was, ran, and biked until I could compete with him and win. The marriage lasted sixteen years. I fought battles and won, more importantly, I stood up for myself and insisted that indeed I was smart, capable, strong, and good-willed. I was ready to move on, or at least I thought so.

My divorce promised a new beginning, a new chapter in my life in which I was to be free, happy, independent, self-sufficient. Several years intervened before I was to realize that life. I know now that a new life does not begin until the old one grows sick and dies, like death from cancer, slowly and painfully. As distant as one may think they are from their spouse, a rope that binds you together twines ever stronger with each passing year. I had to disentangle myself from my old life and grieve the loss.

Soon after leaving my husband, I began to feel as though I had fallen down a deep well. A dark, cold, dank, place, I would scrabble up the slippery wall to climb out. But with fingers torn and bleeding, I would fall back into the muck and lie there miserably weak and defeated. Grief and loss consumed me in the darkest depression I ever hope to know. Loss of what? Of whom? I demanded to know. The hopes and dreams, the loss of youth to a loveless marriage, of social status and wealth? Or of something more sinister, perhaps? The pathological fight with mother, the need to be a victim, sick emotional dependence? In truth, I loved the part of him that was strong, gifted, intelligent, charming, accomplished, and humorous. But he couldn't fully believe in his own capabilities, rather he demanded power, wealth, and status for validation. That he had to belittle me, control me, and stand on my shoulders to make himself tall, demanded that I pull myself away from him to thrive and provide a healthy life for my children.

I felt a deep, inexplicable cavern of loss. I had convinced myself I didn't need anyone, for whom did I have? I didn't love my husband, nor did he love me. I could manage my own affairs, keep up my house, yard, and car, pay my bills, and care for my children. Those things were indeed easier without a man. The revelation that I did need someone, that I needed to love and be loved in return was a difficult one to accept, for it wasn't something I could just go out and buy or make happen at will.

Many suitors passed by me during my years in the well. Some spent nights or weekends, some tried to help, others just didn't care. I looked up to them for help, but knew they could only throw me a rope, that ultimately I'd have to climb out myself. I called upon the strengths I developed as a child, or maybe had been endowed with at birth. I started racing in triathlons. The more I raced, the stronger, happier, and more confident I became. I biked and ran, images of beating the boys on my block, my heels kicking up to my buttocks, spurring me on. But I struggled in the swim portion of the triathlons. I seemed to remain stuck at an earlier stage of development while swimming, never having advanced past intermediate lessons, past the elementary breaststroke. The breaststroke, a slow one compared to freestyle, seemed to be a default mode I could not override. But I ran and biked fast enough to make up for it and earn metals in my age division. More importantly, I developed the strength, skill, and energy to pull myself out of the well.

I met a kind, caring gentleman, who did not pull me out of the well, but cleansed my wounds and nourished my soul. I love and am loved in return. The strong-willed child in me lives on, but I am grown up now, mature, insightful. Never again will I be in an abusive relationship. I have learned my lessons, I have changed.

But my transformation is not complete. Barrett carries on a legacy, playing the roles of his father and grandmother. And there are other things: Unaccountable feelings of anger and resentment, self-recriminations and guilt, pleasure in fighting with my ex-husband, a need to nap more often than I'd like. Just as I need swimming lessons to learn the freestyle stroke, I still need living lessons in some things.

When I bought my older son a car with a manual transmission, I was surprised to find how easily I could drive it, having driven a car with an automatic transmission for at least fifteen years. I didn't have to think about it, I just did it. But when it came time to teach him how to shift and use the clutch, I realized that I unconsciously made a number of mistakes, like riding the clutch around a corner and to a stop sign, rather than downshifting to slow down. Only with a great deal of conscious effort to overcome the learned, routine response, could I reprogram my feet and hands to do it right.

Such is my task in relationships now. I need to consciously reprogram unconscious, unnecessary responses learned long ago, lest they wear out the clutch and breaks of my new life. So what am I doing wrong with Barrett? Granted he is his father's son, genetically and behaviorally, and mine. But what reflexive, destructive actions sabotage my relationship with my son? What still lies below the surface of my consciousness? What remnants of the past still drive my feelings and actions to play dramatic reruns of an old soap opera?

When the police arrive, Barrett has disappeared. The two men in blue uniforms, pistols on one hip and black radios on the other, prowl around the house just like in the movies. I look under beds and into cupboards wondering if he's still small enough to hide in such places. Usually I can hear him rustling and breathing or stifling a cough when he hides.

"We've searched the house, he's not here," an officer concludes.

"Barrett?" I call out anyway. "It's not going to do any good to hide."

"Where would he go?"

"His dad's."

"Where does his father live?"

I give directions and look in the garage for Barrett's bicycle. It is still there.

One officer stays to get my story and write a report, while the other prowls the neighborhood looking for Barrett. As we descend the stairs to the family room, Barrett steals across the room, into a storage basement, back to his hiding place under the stairs. I try not to laugh at how clever he's been.

"Son, you come out of there now. I have to talk to you." The officer's face is a mask, his voice a trumpet, he smells of oil, leather, and after-shave, and is closer to Barrett's age than to mine. "Come here now, resisting an officer is a criminal offense."

Barrett resists anyway.

Doesn't he know this kid's oppositional defiant?

The officer tries using a kinder voice. "Come on, I just want to talk to you."

Barrett crawls out; he's probably hungry and uncomfortable, crouched over like that for so long. He's surprisingly truthful in his accounting of events. He scrunches up his face a few times, tosses his head, shrugs his shoulder, and rubs his nose vigorously. I want to cry because I know his tics are constant aggravations, like random electric shocks that cause him to twitch and jerk.

"She grounded me for no reason, so it's her fault."

"You were pounding on the table and swore at me and called me names when I asked you if I could help." I defend myself.

"I can't help it."

"You can pound on a pillow or cardboard box, not the table. You can swear, but not at people."

The officer intervenes. "Your mother had reason to ground you. Parents have a right to discipline their children. This is the third time we've been here. The District Attorney will look more closely at this this time. You can't keep breaking things and pushing your mother around. We could charge you with property damage and domestic assault. You'll probably have to come before the judge and he'll want you to get treatment."

"I won't go."

"Then they'll come to the home. A family therapy treatment team will come to the house."

Treatment. This is what I want to hear. I want to reach him, to ask him how he feels, to ask him to tell me what is wrong and to get an answer. I just want to communicate with him. I just want to help him. I didn't have to call the police, he didn't beat me, bruise me, make me bleed. I seized the opportunity, wrong or right, to stop his use of intimidation and threat against me as well as his future wife and children. I orchestrated this, pushed when I could have withdrawn, called foul when I could have ignored the insults, demanded a stop to destruction when it would have been easier to just keep cleaning up the mess. I have overridden the default mode in my brain that wants to ignore it, run from it, deny its existence, the automatic mode that would perpetuate, even invite a perpetrator-victim relationship with a loved one.

I diligently study life's instruction manual. To override default modes, we must first find them, know where they are, and know when they go into operation. Then we need to decide on the settings we want to enter and save them into memory. It's a deliberate, conscious process; one must pay close attention to, lest we lapse back into old familiar operations of feeling and behaving.

My gentleman lover is not in my life to hurt or use me, of that I am certain for I made a conscious choice that the only man in my life would be a good one, that fighting old battles was over for me. Still it takes time to trust that a man is with me for reasons that are healthy and genuine and that there isn't some hidden troll underneath a kind persona. Harder to stop is the criticism I lay upon myself when there is no one else around to pick at me, as though the old voices keep singing their refrain in my head.

What living lessons do I still need to take? What part of our genetic makeup, Barrett's and mine, lie at the foundation of our existence, immovable, impenetrable, unwieldy? What must I accept in him and him in himself as blood and bone, unbreakable, unstoppable, vital to his existence? What valuable traits and talents need succor to grow, develop, and predominate over the destructive ones? Which plants are flowers to fertilize and water and which plants are weeds to stomp out? Barrett will, with patience and persistence, if not force, with determination and some luck, learn to develop and fully incorporate into his personality the gentle side to his character so often seen by teachers, friends, and relatives.

I envision two family therapists coming to our home, a man, and a woman. We will sit around the aqua green laminate covered breakfast nook, coffee mugs in hand, Barrett chugging low-fat chocolate milk out of a quart bottle. He will offer them cheese and crackers as is his custom when we have guests he wants to please. My older son will be there, though he doesn't want to be, but not my gentleman lover, though he might like to be, because I don't want the soil of past relationships to muddy this one. I want to reserve him for peaceful, joyous times.

They will ask my older son if he thinks family therapy is a good idea. He will nod and look at the floor.

"Why?"

"Because he's a pain in the ass around my friends. He's always breaking things."

"Like what?"

"Like my CD's . . . video game controllers. He's broken a ton of those." He'll glance at me, then his little brother, and then go back to looking at the floor.

Our cats, Betty Lou and Billy Bob, will watch every move, turning their heads from one person to another, then lick a tail or paw before going back to watching the stage play in our kitchen. "How would you like things to be different? What would you like to see happen?"

I will pause for a sip of coffee, but they will wait and listen. "I want to be able to help him when he's mad. I want to go downstairs when he's in a fury over a video game, suggest that maybe he try something else for a while and not have him swear or throw something at me. When I ask him what's wrong, to hear him tell me that he's angry, or frustrated, that he can't stop himself from trying to win the game, or that his tics bother him, and to some how comfort him and have that help. I want to tell him what a neat kid he is, how smart and creative, without having him mimic and laugh at me. I want him to be happy, to like himself, to not provoke his older brother. I want him to take piano lessons."

Then they will ask Barrett what he wants and he will look straight at me, take my hand in his, and say, "I want the same thing."

And then I will tell them this story about Barrett:

When my father was hospitalized with severe pancreatitis three years ago, Barrett became quite disturbed when he heard the news. He needed to see grandpa immediately. When I entered my father's room, my feet became numb, then my hands and mouth, an old primitive response I thought I'd gotten rid of long ago. I sat down on a beige vinyl-padded lounge chair, took slow deep breathes, then removed the gum in my mouth because I could no longer find it's location with my tongue. I'd worked in a hospital for over ten years, but it had not served to desensitize me, but rather to numb me.

Five green and clear plastic tubes ran in and out of my father's body, out of his nose into the wall, from under the bed into a yellow bag, from needles in his hands into a computer box on a metal stand. Thin, pale, and white-haired, he grew white stubble of beard, something I'd never seen on my father. Dried blood crusted over his bruised hands and arms, heavy white adhesive keeping the IV's in place. A thin cotton gown and sheet barely covered his purple feet.

Without a word, Barrett crawled into his grandpa's bed, pulling a white mesh blanket over their legs, and then snuggled up under my father's arm, lying his head down on his chest. "I love you, grandpa."

"I love you too, Barrett."

The two dozed together, old and young, vital and weak, the wizened and unpretentious. In the corridor, newspapers rumbled on carts, the smell of overcooked food mingled with antiseptic and medicinal remedies. Room freshener fought with bodily secretions. Flowers arrived. The bright summer sun rode across the sky through a wall-size pane of glass.

When visiting hours ended, Barrett kissed his grandfather, and slid out of his hospital bed, carefully, so as not to pull on any needles or tubing. He picked up chalk from a metal trough under a green slate board on the wall that the doctor's and nurses used to write information for the patient, like names of staff and medications. Barrett printed his name in well-formed block letters on the board followed by the telephone numbers of his mother's house and his father's house. He drew a picture, a stick figure of himself with a word balloon over it like you see in comic books, with the inscription: 'I love you, grandpa.' Lastly, he printed, MS. JOHNSTON, RM. 221, LAKEWOOD ELEMENTARY SCHOOL, 223-3166.

"Grandpa, if you need me for anything, anything at all, call me anytime in the middle of the night or during the day. You can reach me during the day at Lakewood School, just ask for Ms. Johnston's room, and ask for Barrett."

Somewhere inside this young man is a child of caring and compassion, a gentle soul, a budding musician, a potential computer genius. His hard drive came with intelligence and sensitivity, anger and mercy, determination and frustration, ferocity, love, hate, affection, and passion. With each new challenge in his life, each new passage, each new program, he has a default mode, which he can use or override. The operating modes he chooses and how he overrides the destructive ones are tasks we share. As his mother, I strive to teach him, support him, rein him in when needed, and love him no matter what.

The Libra Soul
Edward Delgado-Romero & Amy Heesacker

Ed's story:

Having spent the eight years of our relationship trying not to get Amy pregnant, it struck me as an odd experience at age 33 to be doing otherwise. In this case the flesh was willing, but the spirit was ambivalent. Other people, mostly friends and family as well as the occasional stranger, felt very comfortable telling us that we should have kids by now. Everyone told us that we would make perfect parents and what a shame it was that we didn't have children. Although everyone else thought I was ready to be a parent, I wasn't so sure. I felt unprepared and immature. I was successful, in that I had my doctorate, was happily married and financially secure. Yet being a father was something I wasn't sure I could do. I was a great uncle, but being a father seemed like an entirely different job description.

Given that Amy and I are both over-achieving first children, we found out she was pregnant after the first month of trying. Amy was so happy she was radiant. She immediately told her family, my family, our friends, salespeople and other complete strangers. I am a much more private person than Amy (some even say I'm secretive), so I found her openness unnerving. Amy insisted that I tell our co-workers, which I felt was a major violation of my boundaries. I felt acutely uncomfortable talking about highly personal issues with others, but it made Amy happy so I went along with it.

I did feel happy, especially for Amy, but I mostly felt very scared and concerned. One night I made the mistake of watching a program on the Discovery channel that graphically displayed what happened during pregnancy, from the inside. The main point of the show was that it was a miracle that any being survived the rigors of intense biological battle that was pregnancy. I sat wide-eyed and watched in horror as millions of sperm died in the hostile environment of the uterus. That night the sperm massacre was in my nightmare.

Amy went out and bought every book she could get her hands on about pregnancy. It seemed like she wanted to find out the reason behind every sensation that she was feeling. She encouraged me to read the books, but at that point more data and details about things that could go wrong were the last things I needed to know. I found myself having to consciously suspend my fears and concerns. It seemed to me that pregnancy was an exercise in denial, denial that anything could go wrong. As I looked around all I could see were people with newborns. All kinds of people had children: teens, smokers, and abusive parents, even starving people in Africa. Certainly Amy and I would be able to have one too. However I also thought about a person I knew whose baby had died in delivery or a person I knew whose baby died of SIDS.

Amy kept me informed of every new sensation, ache and pain. I went with her to all her pre-natal appointments, but I almost fainted when the doctor gave her a standard gynecological exam. I guess I had to get used to a closer relationship with reproductive biology. During my first visits I felt stupid sitting there as I looked at the people in the waiting room, almost everyone was younger than I was. I wondered if I was developmentally delayed for waiting so long to have a baby. However, slowly I lost some of my defensiveness. We had a lot to look forward to: sonograms, heartbeats and pregnancy classes.

Amy's story:
          Shortly after I found out that I was pregnant my sister-in-law, Maria, E-mailed me the name of a web site that contains "baby horoscopes." The web site provides astrological personality information about babies based on their birth date or due date. Maria shared how the horoscopes had accurately predicted my nephew's sensitivity to frustration and my niece's propensity for diva-like behavior. I was appropriately impressed with her account and excited to uncover the secrets of my unborn child.
          I have always been intrigued by astrology, in that the profiles on Pisces have seemed to describe me to a "T" (e.g., "a see-saw of emotions," "compassionate to a fault," "extremely invested in relationships"). Of course I have often chosen to disregard the adjectives that did not fit me so neatly (e.g., "creative and artistic," "free-spirited"). My husband, Ed, and I had even had an acquaintance create a couple's star chart for us. My memory of the chart is that it described each of our strengths and weaknesses embarrassingly well and suggested that we were nearly a perfect match. Ed, the Scorpio, was accurately characterized as a passionate yet skeptical individual who could be counted on to be emotionally strong, a nice compliment to my Pisces style.
          Based on my rewarding experience with horoscopes in the past and my gripping desire to know something personal about this

baby I was carrying inside of me, I quickly jumped at the chance to use the web site my sister-in-law suggested to me. Due Date: October 5, 2000. I racked my brain to remember if I had ever known anyone with an early October birthday. Ed's birthday was later in the month so I figured the sign was likely to be different. Our friend Carlos informed us that his birthday is October 5. As usual, I had not remembered a friend's birthday, perhaps a trademark of a creative, free-spirited Pisces. How would I describe my friend Carlos? He is thoughtful, caring, sensitive and extremely hard working, but possibly his most attractive trait is his quick sense of humor. Would our baby be like Carlos? The thought made me happy.

The web site indicated that our Libra baby would be friendly, easy-going and creative. Maybe this baby would embody the creativeness I had longed for and captured in my husband. Perhaps our baby would be a painter or an actor or a musician. I speculated that our baby was going to be one of those children that is quietly and wonderfully amazing to care for and know. The baby horoscope profile surprised me by suggesting that our baby would have difficulty making decisions and would require ample time and space to learn to make independent choices. Ed and I are careful and worried about most of the decisions that we make, but we certainly have not found decision making to be overly difficult for us. We tend to always be on a forward moving path, achieving most of what we plan to achieve and then moving on. Perhaps this would be our opportunity to slow down a bit and take the time to feel less pressured about the next step. We would be forced to be less ambitious with our baby and take the time to let this little person find his or her own way. Oh, I loved that.

Ed's story:

One of the more interesting side effects of pregnancy that I experienced was that I felt a peculiar slowing down of my life. I had been promoted to assistant director of our counseling center in only three years and had lived my life in one big blur of activity. I rarely had a moment that went unfilled. But now I felt like everything slowed down, that every moment seemed to count more. I shared this feeling with my friend Bob and he wrote back:

> I appreciate and resonate with the contents of your message. I thought that your perception of "time moving slowly" now that Amy is pregnant was an accurate description of a process that is defined by the arrival and passage of each pre-natal day. Your wife is visibly

changing right before your eyes, and the baby's development and imminent arrival is right out there in the forefront; no pun intended. Apprehension? Oh yeah, just a little bit I'd say. The real issues in human existence are those which pertain to birth and death themselves, and because of their power and meaning, put us in a space where we realize how little we actually do control.

Bob, a proud father of two, was one of the few people that I could talk with about my apprehension and fears. I felt that if I was open about my feelings with anyone else that it would be selfish or bring bad luck. Most of the attention was appropriately focused on Amy at this time, so it was good to have Bob with whom I could share what I was feeling.

Amy and I also changed our schedules, in that we stayed at home more and spent more time together. This was a welcome development. Amy lost her appetite and started giving me at least half of each meal. We stopped exercising and going to our martial arts classes. I started to gain a lot of weight. This was not a welcome development. Soon I began to experience severe back pain. I was taking sympathy pains to a new level.

In our excitement we had gone out and bought a video camera and a new computer that would allow us to make movies. Our first movie was about our first visit to the doctor. I transferred the movie to a CD-ROM and gave it to our families. I began to relax and caught myself thinking and dreaming about the baby. Amy would update me daily and often show me pictures of little alien looking creatures that were supposed to look like my baby. One of the things that we spent a lot of time doing was coming up with names. We finally decided on names that would reflect the names of the important people in our lives and would reflect both of our ethnic heritages. The day after we told our families the names we had come up with, the unimaginable happened.

Amy's Story:
March 24, 2000: The day I found out that my baby had died.

When my baby should have been 12 weeks along, I noticed a little spotting and called the doctor to check it out. It was after regular working hours, so the doctor called me back after she was paged. I really expected her to tell me that everything was probably all right and we would just meet at our regularly scheduled appointment in another week. I had several friends and family members who had experienced bleeding during their pregnancies, and they had subsequently delivered perfectly healthy babies to hold and nurture and love. But instead of reassuring me that all was well with the world, the doctor asked me to come into the office the next morning. The only thing that I remember her saying during the phone call is that "bleeding is never normal during a pregnancy."

Oh God! How was I going to sleep all night with that thought in my head? Somehow I was able to calm myself with the thought of my friends and family members who had successfully overcome the abnormality of this situation and with the incredibly naïve thought that if this was a miscarriage…it was probably meant to be. How stupid! Meant to be? How can a baby dying be meant to be? Dying after playing chicken with a freight train makes sense…but this was not supposed to happen. Ed and I spoke very little that night. I think both of us were too scared to speak about the possibilities.

I drove Ed in to work when we learned that there would be an extended wait to get in to see the doctor. She was busy delivering a baby. When Ed got out of the car he gave me a kiss as he always does, and he told me to call him as soon as I knew anything. I knew that Ed was worried and I knew that he thought we would learn the worst had happened, but he just told me to call him. Neither of us said much of anything about anything that morning. I don't remember the drive back to the doctor's office. I just remember the waiting room with all the pregnant women in it. There were babies of all different ages and women with large round bellies. I placed my hands on my small belly as I had many times over the past three months, and I tried to imagine a little tiny version of a baby all warm and cozy in a sac of nurturing liquid. However, I could not see the baby in my mind because the throbbing pulse of my heartbeat in my temples was drowning all my attempts at serene thought out.

Finally after an excruciating wait the nurse called my name and followed me back to an office without a door. She quickly asked me about the bleeding and took my blood pressure. It seemed that she was rushing through the questions this morning and that made me even more nervous. Doesn't she want more information? What about all the normal pregnancy questions, like: How have you been eating? How have you been feeling? Are you starting to show? This is still a pregnancy, right? So why the rush? Next was the scale. I said a silent prayer that the scale would not betray me. Oh good, up two pounds. That's good, right? Isn't that good? Why isn't she telling me that this is good?

Next I was whisked back to the examination room. There I sat for what seemed like an hour covered by a paper sheet that made too much noise with my frequent fidgets. I remembered a similar feeling the day that I had laid on a harder table waiting to have a doctor check the results of an ultrasound for a breast lump. I remembered that I had told myself on that occasion, "This is it. In the next few minutes you will either find out something that will change your life forever, or you will find out something that will be quickly forgotten." That moment had been quickly forgotten when the bump turned out to be nothing, and I tried to tell myself that this moment would be the same. I stared out the window overlooking the City of Trees and imagined that I was hearing the baby's heartbeat and moving on to the next stage of this wonderful adventure.

Tap, Tap, Tap. The door. Oh God. My doctor smiled sweetly and said that she planned to listen for the baby's heartbeat since at 12 weeks the timing is right. I told her that I had been hoping she would, and I was only sorry that my husband would not be with me for this beautiful event.

Whaw, Whaw, Whaw. A heartbeat. I smiled at the doctor expectantly, but she did not smile back and said that what I heard was my own heartbeat. She moved the little heartbeat machine across my belly just like the countless women I had watched enviously on The Learning Channel show "A Baby Story." Oh why was there nothing coming through? I strained my ears to hear something that the doctor couldn't. It's there; I know it's there. I heard it in my dreams. I thought I even felt it under my fingers the other night as I lay awake in bed and fantasized about our friendly little soul.

Suddenly the doctor stopped trying and said that she would now be doing a pelvic exam to see how everything looked. Oh God. As she put on her rubber gloves she asked me if my waist had been disappearing, a sign that the uterus was growing to accommodate the little fetus. Oh yes, I was wearing clothes with elastic waistbands these days just for that reason. I remembered Ed and I giggling in the dressing room of a department store as I modeled my first maternity pants with an ample pouch for later. Yes, I was definitely growing and proudly sharing all the other signs that proved I was pregnant even without the tummy.

"Amy, I'm worried about this pregnancy," the doctor said. "This might be a miscarriage."

"Okay" I said back.

I don't know why I said, "Okay." There was nothing 'Okay' about this situation or about the statement from the doctor. My head was leaving my body then, and it was entering a large tunnel that got smaller and smaller as it floated away from me. Then there was a rush of movement again and thoughts and more statements. We need to go next door for an ultrasound. You will have to go back to the waiting room while I prepare it for you.

The waiting room again. There were more pregnant women this time, and each one of them turned to me and made eye contact. I must have been as pale as that noisy paper sheet by the time I made it to my seat because each of them looked away quickly without a smile. Should I call Ed? What do I tell him? She didn't say that this was a miscarriage, did she? This is just a small baby. It was just one of those cases where the doctor can't find the heartbeat right away. Maybe I was off on my calculation of the due date. Maybe this isn't a Libra baby after all. Maybe, just maybe, this is all going to be one of those moments that gets forgotten.

The doctor came out herself this time to call my name. I didn't think that was a good sign. On the way down the hall I noticed a nurse answering questions for an expectant couple and a woman taking payments from patients with newborn infants. It was busy and bright with lots of large bellied women to make way for. The room with the ultrasound machine was small and filled almost entirely by the large computer attached. There was a bed for me to lie on and a monitor for me to watch. The doctor seemed calm and made small talk with me as she got everything going. I saw her moving the wand across my uterus, searching, searching. My monitor didn't work that day. It was a large black screen that looked down at me reflecting my own petrified face.

When the doctor turned her screen so that I could see the picture, I couldn't catch a breath. One cold tear rolled down the side of my turned face and into my ear. The picture revealed a sac for a baby filled with nothing but blackness. I felt that blackness seep out of the monitor and into my eyes sockets and down into my belly and even deeper into my soul. It was gone. My dreams of mushy, smooth skin to cradle between my neck and shoulder were gone with it.

I want Ed and I want him now.

The next thing I remember is running across the street to the parking garage. The tears were searing the inside of my eyelids, but I was determined to make it to the car before they burst over the edges. It was too late. As I reached the cement stairwell all I could see were curvy shapes in the dark shadows as my tears warped the scenery. I had to make it to the car and call Ed. He had to know this right now. Somehow I found my way to the car without running into anybody and I plunked myself down in the passenger seat. I remember having the strange thought that I didn't want any other patients to get their hopes up by thinking that I was pulling out of the nearly full lot. Why did I care about that?

"University Counseling Center," the secretary said cheerfully, "How may I help you?"

"I need to talk to Ed," I managed to squeak into the cell phone.

"Amy?" She asked in a concerned tone, "What's wrong?"

That was it. I could say no more. No words, no sound. Nothing.

"I'll get him right now, Hon," she said in a reassuring yet pressured voice, "Just hang on."

Ed's story:

The night before I hadn't slept. I lay next to Amy terrified. I knew she was awake as well, but we couldn't say anything. The next morning I had Amy drop me off at work. It was the first time that I didn't go with her to an appointment because we had job interviews at work and I had to be there. Although this was true, not going was a way for me to deny what was going on. Perhaps by some miracle it would just be a routine checkup and we would both laugh that we were such typical nervous first-time parents.

When the phone rang during an interview I knew what had happened. I walked down to my office and before I picked up the phone I knew. I knew.

Amy's story:

I can still account for every moment of the rest of that day. It must have been the summer solstice because it seemed that the day had no end. There was the drive to pick up Ed. There were the phone calls from friends checking in about my morning appointment. There was the decision to have the D&C and the waiting to hear that it had been scheduled. There was the blood test and the infuriating hospital form that had the nerve to strip away any last ounce of denial about what was happening.

Are you pregnant? Yes or No?

I wanted to rip up that cheerfully colored form and throw it at the woman across the desk. Yes, I was pregnant only a few hours ago, but no, I don't think that I am anymore.

The day that never ended lasted all night long. I laid on the couch with a heating pad for my cramping uterus. Every pain shot darts into my heart, piercing holes in the fresh layer of confidence that had come from knowing I was a mother and held a precious baby inside of me. Ed slept restlessly on the floor beside me as I changed the channels in the dark. I couldn't bear to watch a scary movie or news about violence in other countries. Everything I watched seemed too intense, too negative and too close to my own experience. I tried turning the television off several times, but the silence would attack me like an imaginary monster from under the bed. My ears would fill with leftover sound as if I had just left a noisy rock concert. But instead of musical memories my mind would flood with the events of the day and the thoughts of what I had lost. With the television back on I finally settled on a movie about young love and fell briefly into an uneasy sleep.

Thankfully, Ed handled all the phone calls for the first few days. I didn't have to tell anyone, but I listened carefully to see how Ed was going to handle it. I know he was sad, but he just kept repeating that he needed to take care of me. In the days and weeks that followed, I recognized on a spiritual level how important Ed had become to me. He did everything right and nothing wrong. He listened as I talked incessantly about my pain, fear, sadness, and anger. He validated every emotion and every thought, often sharing that he had been experiencing the very same things. I felt so well cared for that I began to feel guilty asking so much of him. However, I did not feel that I had the strength to act bravely at this time so I gave in to the weight of my emotions and leaned heavily upon him.

Ed's story:

The next few hours and days seemed like a slow-motion nightmare. My back pain intensified to excruciating levels and I was unable to move without a great deal of pain. I didn't mind, it was oddly comforting to have some physical pain to focus on. Despite my pain, both physically and emotionally, I had to take care of Amy and also start notifying all of our family and friends. I felt guilty every time I called someone to tell him or her the news. I remember feeling like I was floating around the hospital as I waited for Amy to get out of her D&C. The fact that it was a beautiful sunny day just made everything worse.

Amy slept throughout most of the following days. We were so lucky that our friends dropped their lives, and literally fed us and took care of us for a few days. I'm not sure what we would have done without their generosity. Amy decided to go back to work the next Monday and we had a professional conference to attend the next weekend. It seemed like a good idea to get out of town.

With the same fervor that she had taken to learning about pregnancy, Amy set about learning about miscarriages. She was determined to do everything right. I felt she was pushing herself too hard and had unrealistic expectations for when and how she should feel better. The doctor had been very helpful and caring, but not overly so. She explained that the baby had "dissolved," that there was nothing that we had done wrong, and that in fact miscarriage was very common. We found this to be true as almost everyone we talked to had experienced a miscarriage or knew someone who did. The openness about our pregnancy helped because soon everyone knew about the miscarriage and Amy got a lot of support from people. However it also meant that every time someone who didn't know about the miscarriage approached us we were re-traumatized by having to tell the person the bad news and then feeling somehow responsible for hurting them. The worst feeling was when people who didn't know would touch Amy's belly as they asked her how she was doing. Somehow the physical touch just made things all the more real. This went on for months.

Amy's story:
        I came to find, as one day pulled itself slowly into the next that the time immediately following the miscarriage was actually easier to cope with than the time that came after. As a psychologist, I had developed the ability to identify all the appropriate feelings associated with a crisis and determine the appropriate course of action to follow. In my case I knew that feeling sad, mad and confused was appropriate so I let myself experience these feelings without guilt or limits. I found all the appropriate people to care for me and talk with me. I read an incredibly validating book and learned from the lessons of the authors. As a psychologist I understood the importance of this time for healing and I jumped into it knowingly and willingly.
        What I was not expecting was the extended period of depression and anxiety that followed the initial crisis period. The dependable coping strategies that had served me well through years of graduate training and the daily hassles and life stressors that everyone experiences were not working for me anymore. I continued to have sleepless nights, deep resentment toward women with children, and a free-floating anxiety that was not easy to pin down or address. I saw

myself as a different person, and I did not necessarily like what I saw. I felt extremely vulnerable, insecure, self-conscious and incompetent during this time. Luckily for me, I had a sensitive and extremely supportive husband who heard and understood my neediness at that time. Ed and I had started looking for a house to buy shortly after we learned about the pregnancy. When the miscarriage occurred the idea of spending money for more space seemed overindulgent and risky to me. However, not going ahead with the plan also felt like another loss, at a time when I needed to feel that I was making some headway and accomplishing one of my goals. Ed agreed, and we found a home to make our own with a special room reserved for an eventual nursery. Ed thought that it was important to paint the room yellow before we moved in, perhaps the color of hope for our future.

Ed's story:

I dealt with my loss by protecting Amy and by being angry. I found myself filled with rage and unable to tolerate large group interactions and meetings. There were a few instances when I lost my temper, which was not very typical of my work style. I shut myself in my office and I hid from everyone that I knew. I did a good job of convincing people that I had dealt with the miscarriage, too good. I later found myself resenting the fact that I didn't feel much support from my colleagues. I was especially angry when colleagues couldn't connect my anger with my loss.

My fear was that I was somehow to blame; that perhaps it had been my fault the baby was not viable. Was it something defective about my sperm? Was I to blame for inflicting this pain on my wife? If I gave voice to these fears would I be stealing the spotlight from Amy?

I also found myself avoiding newborns and being especially angry with teenage mothers or absent fathers. I developed a hatred for the Dilley sextuplets and their stupid parents who were so greedy that they had six children at one time while I had none. Mostly I was angry with God who let things like this happen, and I recoiled when anyone would mention, "things happen for a reason." There was no reason I could see for hurting like this. I insisted that Amy and I should continue with our plans to buy a house and create our nest. I believed that we would not let our recovery from this loss hinge on a successful pregnancy. I felt it was unfair to ask a baby to heal the broken heart of his father.

I still struggle to make sense of this loss, and I battle with the pessimism and negativity that I use to protect myself. I still have hope that I will have the chance to be a good father. Perhaps this little soul taught me never to take anything for granted and to treasure the people I love. Perhaps this loss will make me a much better father because I know what it is was like to lose a part of me. Perhaps I'll be a better husband because I now know what a strong woman my wife is. Perhaps our dreams have been postponed rather than destroyed...

Our baby's Libra soul touched our lives in important ways. Perhaps our little Libra had some difficulty making the decision to be born on our schedule. Our Libra's indecisiveness forced us to re-evaluate our achievement focus and challenged our beliefs about how much control we actually have over such things. This baby provided us with the opportunity to slow down and take the time to experience the next step in all its lovely excitement and moments of painful reflection.

Hope: A Quantitative Analysis

George S. Howard & Edward A. Delgado-Romero

Hope lies in the way one tells a story. The authors of this collection of essays realize that one can speak of terrible events—racism, depression, sexism, miscarriages, death, oppression and abuse of many kinds—and if one tells the tale properly, there is hope. And why is hope important?

The book of Proverbs says simply, "Hope deferred maketh the heart sick" (13:12). The real enemy in all the stories recounted in this book is despair, not the nominal opponents against whom (or which) the authors struggled. One cannot beat racism, homophobia, or death in any conventional way. Rather, one struggles valiantly against the insidious effects that occur when one despairs and fights no more. None of the authors will completely defeat their problems in their lifetimes. And from George Howard's perspective as a Catholic educator, only one human is said to have escaped death—while another demonstrated His conquest over death by raising himself and others from the dead. Thus, the rest of us are condemned to struggle against various adversaries without the hope of total victory. Rather, we must hope for the more restricted victory—to have conquered the demons of bitterness and despair that can corrupt a life of struggle without hope.

The book begins with George Howard exploring the possibility of his death if he did not overcome his depression and reluctance to get help. By imagining what could happen, both positively and negatively, George was able to find hope and therefore the energy to overcome his inertia and get help for his condition. That doesn't mean that the death scenario will not happen – it will happen eventually. However George may have been able to prolong his life for quite some time and the quality of that life has most likely been improved. Similarly Mike Murphy in his chapter described "a crushing, gut-wrenching depression" in response to problems with his son and his need to be perfect. Perfectionism is a cruel and unyielding master. Many of the authors talk in detail about struggling with their own internal expectations of perfection.

Both George and Mike were able to turn to healers, a medical doctor and therapist respectively, and both were able to find meaning in their suffering and improve the quality of their lives. That doesn't mean that George won't die or that Mike won't continue to experience difficulties with his son. However they were both able to find hope to continue on. One of the qualities of despair is that it drains energy and sends one into a downward spiral. In contrast, hope breathes energy and possibility.

Hope crackles throughout the authors' narratives. Amy Heesacker traces the path of her hope as it relates to her career path and the constant revisions to her path. At first she looks outwardly for answers, and over time internalizes the wisdom of others along with developing wisdom of her own. She learns to value the flexibility of her path rather than fighting against perceived constraints and the loss of her perfect plan. For example, rather than focusing on the grisly and morbid details of her work evaluating sex offenders, Amy focuses on the fact that she is helping to protect children by ensuring these offenders stay incarcerated. In this way she finds meaning rather than despair. Amy finds hope for the future rather than dwelling in the past or mourning a fantasized possibility.

Mary Fukuyama also explores her career path, although she is at a different place in her life than Amy. Mary chooses to follow her partner into a foreign land and stripped of the comforts of home, takes the risk of intense self-reflection. She wasn't always happy with what she found (unexpected anger, possessiveness) yet she crossed the river to emerge a changed person. Through her E-mail communication with her colleagues back home she was able to share her experiences and also provide a lifeline for her to return home.

In modern times there seems to be a movement towards declaring problems such as racism and oppression "solved". Many of the authors chose to delve into the reality of racism and oppression in their lives and state emphatically that the problems are not "solved" – far from it. George Howard has what the noted psychologist Janet Helms would term an "encounter" experience as he is faced with several examples that serve to disconfirm the notion that society in general, and his beloved university specifically, has not solved the problem of racism. This dawning awareness spurs him to ask: "what if things are getting worse?" Will George use this insight to try to change things and work towards social justice? Or will despair take root and George choose to re-enter a cocoon of denial?

What happens where despite ones best efforts a friend retreats further into despair and seems to lose touch with reality? Edward Delgado-Romero tells the story about two friends who go in vastly different directions, one becomes a multicultural activist, the other a racist. Although the seeds for both were planted before meeting, their paths briefly cross. Ed is left with self-recrimination; unmet savior fantasies and yet at the same time he manages to find meaning in this failed relationship. Like Mary, Ed was taken out of his comfort zone and he made the choice to more fully examine and live his values.

Max Parker had decided on his values, he was going to work in the north and make money. However, he was tricked into attending college and once there devoted himself to improving himself. Max explicitly talks about the components of his success: that a willingness to help himself drew helpful people to him; that he needed to take risks and be flexible; that he needed to have a spiritual element, a "power beyond" to help him during difficult or seemingly impossible times; and finally that he needed to learn how to live, not simply learn how to make a living. Max's faith and hope, in the face of overwhelming odds, enabled him to not only survive but to thrive. Through his work as a counselor educator he has inspired and helped several generations of students. As an African-American man who grew up in the Deep South and attended a historically Black college, Max's narrative is also infused with the lived experience of race and racism.

Sue Morrow and Jesse Aros take the topics of race, racism, sexism, heterosexism and oppression and run with them. Sue and Jesse not only disclosed embarrassing and powerful moments in their lives, but they also took the risk to challenge each other to go deeper. Sue challenged Jesse about his lingering homophobia and Jesse challenged Sue about her feeling "worthy" enough to hear his story. Rather than driving them apart, the challenges and resulting discussions enable Sue and Jesse to grow closer. Their resolution was the idea that to truly share the pain of another person one had to go beyond "one-upping" each other in an escalating competition of victim hood. One had to acknowledge that sometimes one benefited from oppression (sometimes one is the lamb and sometimes one is the coyote). Therefore, they modeled exactly the kind of process that they wanted the field to undergo: a deep analysis of pain and privilege in the context of a caring relationship. Their hope lies in the expectation that people, especially those in the helping profession, will take the risk to have these types of conversations with each other.

Gargi Roysircar painted her experience with her poetry. Her poems, at first are about differences and divisions. Gargi, who was born in India, sees herself through other's eyes, a "mango tree flourishing in the cornfield". Her poem, *Killing in Religions Name*, which she initially wrote in 1999 ominously foreshadowed the September 11th, 2001 terrorist attacks on the United States (she chose to update the poem for this volume). One can sense the anger, loss and loneliness that centers on racism, poverty and religious strife. However, without any feedback from the editors she wrote us and shared "The three previous poems, through realistic, have a tone of bitterness. In addition, given current conflicts and polarizations around the world, I thought my concerns for social justice should express thoughts on the peaceful co-existence of cultural, religious, and geopolitical differences". Thus her last poem, *On This Same Earth*, is her expression of hope in the face of bitterness. Rather than be consumed by despair and still acutely aware of differences, Gargi finds comfort and hope in commonalities.

Luis Rivas wrote about his experience as a double minority in the United States: a Puerto-Rican born *Isleño* (a person with an identity as a Puerto Rican Islander rather than as a US Hispanic) and a person diagnosed with Attention Deficit Hyperactivity Disorder (ADHD). Luis weaves these two forms of marginalization and minority status to ask the question: "is this a double whammy or a double blessing?" Luis, like many of the other authors in the book, expected more from his professors and colleagues in the helping professions. He expected the compassion and sensitivity that he was trained to give clients and yet did not get it. Luis' experience, Sue being told she was too old for graduate school, Mike's colleagues not responding to his pain, are all examples of helping professionals failing to be empathic with each other. Luis manages to make sense of his double whammy and find the double blessing in his dual minority status; also like many of the other authors in this book, Luis was able to use his experience to become a better counselor.

All of us constantly struggle to find meaning in our lives. For many people children are an obvious, important element to the total contribution that our lives represent. The decision to have children is a life altering decision that some make consciously while others are presented with the reality of a child. Mike Murphy wrote about the kind of parent that he aspired to be; how he always put parenting first. He described having children as having a piece of his heart walking around outside of his body. Thus when his son encountered difficulties he was crushed as discussed earlier. Similarly, an anonymous author talks about the shock in discovering that his son had slid into delinquent behavior much more quickly and deeply than the author thought possible. He realizes that his son is slipping out of his watchful control and finds it frightening. Both of these parents, Mike and the anonymous author, have invested a tremendous amount of themselves in the lives of their sons and both are faced with fear, depression and despair. Both find meaning and grow from their experiences, but the reader will note there is no "happy ending"; both fathers are left with many questions about their abilities as parents and fears for their sons. Yet they have hope that their sons will successfully make the transition into adulthood. What is that hope based upon? In counseling, trainees are often told to "trust the process". Similarly these fathers trust that these issues are part of the process both for their sons and for themselves.

Cindy Anderson Keene provides the story of a mother faced who suddenly realizes and then tries to change the patterns of her life. She uses the metaphor of a computer hard drive both to represent the hard-wired environmental and genetic influences in her life as well as to represent the difficult task of being a parent to her son. Like many parents Cindy finds that the challenges of raising her son bring up her own unresolved issues that she must also contend with. However, unlike most parents Cindy must deal with the fact that her son has Tourettes Syndrome. In the face of abuse Cindy maintains the hope that "I, as his mother, (can) reach down into the deepest part of my spirit to marshal all the will and strength I possess to try to dig out and nourish the kind, gentle character who lives inside at the core of my son." Cindy's challenge is enormous, as is her hope and resolve. Cindy realizes that in taking care of her son, she must take care of herself as well. Despair or selfless martyrdom could be attractive alternatives, yet she chooses to take the hard drive.

Some people have parenthood denied them at some point. Sue Morrow talks about the way that in which her husband took her children from her when she came out as a lesbian. One can feel her outrage as she describes being a "super mom" and doing everything by the book. Yet, when she decided to be true to herself she was forced to pay an inhuman price—her children were taken from her. Sue states "And I, too, learned that the only way to tolerate that level of pain, to lose your babies, was never to cry, never to give in to the pain, to become numb." Yet later Sue used her pain to connect with others in pain and chose to make sense of her pain by becoming an advocate for others in pain.

Edward Delgado-Romero and Amy Heesacker also had their parenthood denied to them. The themes that Amy introduced in her solo chapter are played out further in this story as she is presented with another challenge to her dreams and fantasized life script. After years of postponing parenthood she and Ed decide to have a child and are instead confronted with a miscarriage. They struggle to make sense of their loss, each in their own way. Amy throws herself into healing and Ed is consumed by anger (and fear). They both decide to try again, but are resolved not to let their healing depend on a successful pregnancy. To them hope is more than just getting what you want, it is a belief that eventually things will work out—whatever that may mean. The miscarriage could drive them apart or bring them closer together, once again the choice is between despair and hope, and as Sue and Jesse have pointed out in a different way, the bedrock of hope is a solid relationship.

For some, the choice of having children is precluded. Their challenge, then, is to find other modes to create meaning for themselves. Some create meaning through adoption, lives of service to others, spiritual leadership, creating positive civic institutions, defending the vulnerable, heroically standing against oppression, dedicating lives to the Cardinal virtues (to feed the hungry, clothe the naked, comfort the suffering, etc.), as well as a host of other means. As William James said, "We are spinning our own fates, good or evil, and never to be undone. Every smallest stroke of virtue or of vice leaves its never so little scar... Nothing we do is, in strict scientific literalness, wiped out."

Throughout this analysis we have spoken of choices and courage. Yet we have to be specific about what the choices are. As George has pointed out many times in his scholarly writing, volitional control (free will) is bounded by the external forces at play in our lives. The authors in this book did not have a choice in terms of which difficult situations they had to face, what distinguishes them is the choice they make in how they faced those situations. Much as Frankl said " ".

Death, where is thy sting?

The thought of death and the end of life is often the ultimate cause of despair. How can one find hope in the apparent defeat of death? It seems to us that there are two general approaches to meeting death with something other than despair.

Some people see death as another phase or transition in life. Religions often depict life as a test that determines ones lot in the next life—Buddhists can look forward with hope to their next incarnation, Christians hope for the pleasures of heaven. Death is perhaps the most significant event in the life of a Catholic, for those who manage to meet death while in the state of grace, to them Jesus has promised salvation. The gospel story of Dismus, the Good Thief, guarantees that hope is always possible through an act of repentance. Despite having lived a misspent life, Jesus' last words to Dismus were, "Rejoice, for this day thou shall be with me in paradise."

The second general way that one might find meaning in death lies in its status as the official "closing of the books" (as it were) on ones important life tasks and challenges. Speaking for myself (George), there are three major challenges (or roles) that I have freely chosen in my life—to be a husband, a father, and an educator. I measure my worth as a person, in part; by the way I handle those significant challenges. From time to time, I also come close to making my commitment to society or my commitment to the health of our planet one of my major life commitments. One often sees a person's life commitments in their autobiography. For example, General Douglas McArthur saw his cardinal values in "duty, honor, and country." Father Theodore Hesburgh's choices were "God, country, and Notre Dame." Have you ever explicitly stated your core values? It's a difficult but worthwhile exercise. Try it sometime.

From this second perspective, death becomes a natural point for one to review her or his life vis-à-vis their cardinal values. I think that people often choose to be surrounded by family members as death draws near because family is so often at the center our values. Similarly, most of the tough topics in the essays herein depicted family challenges (e.g., dealing with a violent child, family conflict and depression over a child's behavior) or disturbing brushes with people who espoused values (racism, homophobia, sexism, and other forms of prejudice and oppression) that conflict with ones core values. For me, at death I'll be able to close the books on my life as a husband, father, and an educator. Like all of you, I hope to be able to say, "I have fought the good fight, I have run the good race, I have kept faith…"

Our essays represent honest efforts by many people to see hope in painful experiences; to understand how we grew into the life-values that now define our identity and purpose in life; and to state with Nietzsche that, "that which does not kill me makes me stronger." Our hope is that each of us might be successful in life—but what constitutes success? As mentioned above, ideally each of us chooses a set of cardinal values against which our success will be measured. However, when young people think of success, they often do so in terms of grandiose ambitions and dramatic issues. One senses in the tough topics essays, that over time and with greater experience of life's trials and tribulations, we move closer to Ralph Waldo Emerson's more realistic definition of success in life. "What is success? To laugh often and to love much; To win the respect of intelligent people and the affection of children; To earn the appreciation of honest critics and endure the betrayal of false friends; To appreciate beauty; To find the best in others; To leave the world a bit better, whether by a healthy child, a garden patch, or a redeemed social condition; To know even one life has breathed easier because you have lived; That is to have succeeded."

In my judgment, the essay's authors all have good grounds for hope in Emerson's form of success in life. I trust their good efforts serve to help readers take a small step closer to their own life's goals.

INDEX

other "isms", 66-68;
conflicting values
and, 135; earliest
experiences with, 59-
60; and friendship,
39-42; and hope, 129-
131; of non-
governmental
organizations, 30; in
the North vs. the
South, 45; at Notre
Dame,   33, 34;
people's perceptions
of, 62-63; race:
relations, 35; shaping
us as professionals,
68-69; White folks
confronting, 73-75;
White perspective
about, 62
Religion: in Guatemala,
29; religious bigotry,
33
Rio Dulce River, 19-20
"scorched earth" strategy,
29
"self", nature of the, 34
Sexism: conflicting
values and, 135;
earliest experiences
with, 59; and hope,
129-131; shaping
lives, 53-56; in
student narratives,
33
social justice, 20
spiritual values, 27
Stillman College, 46, 47,
49, 51
Teleographies, 1-3, 5

Tourett's syndrome, 105,
108
United States, pace of life
in, 31

Author Biographies

Edward Delgado-Romero is an assistant professor at Indiana University in the Counseling Psychology and Counselor Education Program. He received his Ph.D. from the University of Notre Dame. He was formerly a clinical assistant professor and assistant director in the counseling center at the University of Florida. His research interests include narrative psychology, race and racism, Latino/a psychology, multicultural psychology and ethics.

George S. Howard is a professor in the counseling psychology department at the University of Notre Dame. He received his Ph.D. from Southern Illinois University, Carbondale. George is a prolific writer and author and has extensively published in many areas of psychology. He is currently the director of the Core program for undergraduates at the University of Notre Dame.

Jesus (Jess) Aros describes himself as "a short, squat, one-handed, *Mestizo* brother and educated peasant with one spouse, four kids, and some debts - fiscal and otherwise". He is also 1) the Director of the Graduate Counseling Programs, 2) Associate Professor of Counseling, and 3) can be reached by "snail" and/or electronic mail at: The School of Education, St Mary's College, Moraga, CA, 94575 <jaros@stmarys-ca.edu>.

Mary A. Fukuyama received her PhD from Washington State University and has worked at the University of Florida Counseling Center for the past 20 years as a counseling psychologist, supervisor and trainer. She is a clinical professor and teaches courses on spirituality and multicultural counseling for the Department of Counselor Education and also the Counseling Psychology Program. She recently co-authored a book, with Todd Sevig, *Integrating Spirituality into Multicultural Counseling* published by Sage Publications. Her practice specialties include working with university students from a developmental perspective, multicultural counseling and training, Her current research interests include conducting a qualitative study on "multicultural expressions" of spirituality.

Amy Heesacker, Ph.D. is a counseling psychologist who received her degree from the University of Notre Dame in 1997. Since that time she has held both clinical (e.g., University of Florida Counseling Center, Independent Practice in Gainesville, Florida) and academic positions (e.g., Adjunct Professor at the University of Florida and Indiana University in Bloomington, Indiana). She has been involved in the evaluation of sex offenders and co-authored a chapter on the topic: Shaw, T. S., Heesacker, A. K., & Delgado-Romero, E. A. (2001). "Implications of sexually violent predator laws for youthful offenders". In A. Schlank (Ed.), *The Sexual Predator: Legal Issues, Clinical Issues, and Special Populations (Volume II)*. Kingston, NJ: Civic Research Institute. Dr. Heesacker currently lives in Bloomington, Indiana with her husband, Ed, and their 2-year old son, Javier.

Cindy Keene has a Graduate degree in Social Work and a PhD in Counseling Psychology from the Univeristy of Wisconsin-Madison. She works as a Clinical Program Director-Psychology at The Milwaukee County Mental Health Complex.

Susan L. Morrow received her Ph.D. in counseling psychology from Arizona State University in 1992. She is currently an associate professor and program director in the counseling psychology program at the University of Utah. She is a feminist multicultural counselor, scholar, and teacher, conducting both research and practice related to adult survivors of child abuse, academic climate for graduate women of color, lesbian/gay/bisexual issues, and feminist therapy. As a qualitative methodologist, she hopes to encourage the discipline to embrace multiple paradigms and research methods that will contribute to a more radical perspective on social issues in counseling.

Michael Murphy is a clinical associate professor and staff psychologist at the University of Florida Counseling Center. He also has a private practice specializing in psychotherapy with teenagers and adults. Michael is very happily married and has two healthy, wonderful sons, ages 17 and 21.

Woodrow M. Parker is a professor in the Counselor Department at the University of Florida in Gainesville, Florida. He has been a faculty member at the University of Florida for 29 year and has been a senior staff member at counseling centers at both the University of South Florida two years and three years at the University of Florida for three years. He is a member of the American Counseling Association and is an active member of AMCD and of ACES, Divisions of ACA. He has published six books, five book chapters, and 46 journal articles on various aspects of Multicultural counseling and development.

Luis Rivas is a senior staff psychologist in the counseling center of Setn Hall University. He is a graduate of Southern Illinois University, Carbondale.

Gargi Roysircar is the Founding Director of the Antioch New England Multicultural Center for Research and Practice (www.multiculturalcenter.org) and Professor in the Department of Clinical Psychology (APA-accredited), Antioch New England Graduate School, Antioch University. She does research on the interface of acculturation and ethnic identity with the mental health of immigrants and ethnic minorities; worldview differences between and within cultural groups; multicultural competencies and training in professional psychology; and multicultural assessment and instrumentation. Her recent co-edited books are: *Multicultural competencies: A guidebook of practices* (Roysircar, Sandhu, & Bibbins, 2003) and *Multicultural counseling competencies 2003: Association for Multicultural Counseling and Development* (Roysircar, Arredondo, Fuertes, Ponterotto, & Toporek, 2003). She is a Fellow of the American Psychological Association (APA) in Division 17 (Society of Counseling Psychology) and Division 45 (Society for the Psychological Study of Ethnic Minority Issues) and a Past President (2001-2002) of the Association for Multicultural Counseling and Development. Gargi Roysircar was awarded the 2002 Extended Research Award of the American Counseling Association. At the Antioch MC Center, she integrates research with clinical services, consultation, and education. Prior to joining Antioch New England in Fall 2000, Gargi Roysircar was a tenured associate professor in the counseling psychology program (APA-accredited) of the Department of Educational Psychology, University of Nebraska-Lincoln, where she began her academic career.